The Population Debate

Independence

Educational Publishers
Cambridge

First published by Independence
PO Box 295
Cambridge CB1 3XP

© Craig Donnellan 1995

British Library Cataloguing in Publication Data
The Population Debate – (Issues for the Nineties Series)
I. Donnellan, Craig II. Series
363.96

ISBN 1 872995 60 8

Printed in Great Britain
at Leicester Printers Ltd
Leicester

Typeset by
Martyn Lusher Artwork, Cambridge

Cover
The cartoon on the front cover is by
the artist, Ken Pyne.

CONTENTS

Introduction

The Population Debate is the twentieth volume in the series: **Issues For The Nineties**. The aim of this series is to offer up-to-date information about important issues in our world.

The Population Debate examines the growing concern about world population. The information comes from a wide variety of sources and includes:

Government reports and statistics
Newspaper reports and features
Magazine articles and surveys
Literature from lobby groups
and charitable organisations.

It is hoped that, as you read about the many aspects of the issues explored in this book, you will critically evaluate the information presented. It is important that you decide whether you are being presented with facts or opinions. Does the writer give a biased or an unbiased report? If an opinion is being expressed, do you agree with the writer?

The Population Debate offers a useful starting point for those who need convenient access to information about the many issues involved. However, it is only a starting point. At the back of the book is a list of organisations which you may want to contact for further information.

*****

Overpopulation?

Optimum population

In theory there is an ideal population size for each country. In economic terms this is the level of population at which income per capita is maximised. This would mean that the most efficient use is being made of the country's resources. However, the 'most efficient' use of resources today may result in a scarcity of resources tomorrow unless new resources are found. Therefore optimum population can be achieved temporarily but may be difficult to keep in balance with resources over the long-term. This definition also assumes that each country is a closed system, yet resources can be imported or exported through trade. Globally speaking however, the world is a closed system.

'The density of population necessary to enable mankind to obtain, in the greatest degree, all the advantages both of co-operation and of social intercourse, has, in all the most populous countries, been attained . . . It is not good for a man to be kept perforce at all times in the presence of his species'. Source: John Stuart Mill, *Principles of Political Economy*, vol 2, London, 1857.

Overpopulation

If a country's population exceeds the optimum it is said to be overpopulated. Consequences of overpopulation may include: unemployment, underemployment, malnutrition, environmental degradation and loss of wildlife, pollution, housing shortages, low living standards, war and racism. However, it is arguable how much these symptoms are caused only by overpopulation and how much they are influenced by other social and economic variables.

By Helen Bird & Helen Kay

Underpopulation

On the other hand, underpopulation suggests a situation where there are fewer people in an area than the given resources could actually support. Australia and Canada until recently considered themselves underpopulated and they actively encouraged immigration, so that untapped resources, particularly land, could be utilized.

Is Great Britain overpopulated? – a personal view

Despite a century of mass emigration, Britain is one of the most densely populated countries in the world, with an extra 45 people being added to the population every day. Yet it is often argued that Britain has reached a happy state of optimum population. In contrast to those countries usually considered to be experiencing population pressure, most people here enjoy an excellent standard of living. The majority of the population have homes and some form of income, and there seems little reason for anyone to go hungry.

But Britain still remains dependent on imported supplies of food and animal feeding stuffs for almost one half of its requirements. It has been estimated that if we had to be self-sufficient in food production, we could only support about 30 million people, as opposed to the present 58 million. If we all became vegetarians then more than 40 million could be supported; battery farming has become necessary because an increasing population with increasing affluence has demanded an increasing quantity of cheap meat. The use of inorganic fertilisers and the farming of fragile soils is also partly due to increasing demands, but we have only recently been alerted to the environmental costs.

Other than coal, gas and oil,

Britain has relatively few natural resources and must rely on the export of manufactured goods and the provision of services to pay for imported food and raw materials. During the colonial era the 'new lands' were able to provide these requirements on favourable terms, but as these countries have become independent and grown in both population size and industrial capacity, they have fewer surpluses to export.

Conflict over land use can be a sign of population pressure. Should the remaining countryside be conserved for recreation? Already national parks and coastal areas are suffering from degradation due to the number of visitors each year. Or should it be made available for new housing estates? Or should it be farmed with modern methods resulting in the loss of more hedgerows, wildlife and local character?

In conclusion, it is clear that Britain is unable to meet all its food and resource needs except through trading. It is also clear that the term 'natural resource' can no longer be confined to standard primary products such as coal, copper or grain. Resources now include clean air or water, stable soils, attractive views and so on. With this extended definition of resources in mind, over-population in Britain becomes a serious issue.

● The above is from *Population – a comprehensive study*, available from Population Concern see page 39 for address details.

Populous nations

The world's two most populous nations, China and India, have joined seven other countries in a pledge with a triple, interlinked purpose: to reduce illiteracy, to lower fertility rates and to achieve higher economic growth. The seven others governments are Indonesia, Nigeria, Brazil, Pakistan, Bangladesh, Mexico and Egypt. Together the nine account for half the world's population and seven of every ten adult illiterates. The declaration calls for the nine governments to wipe out illiteracy among their citizens 'by the year 2000 or at the earliest possible moment'. By signing the four-page declaration at a New Delhi conference entitled 'Education for All', the governments promised to 'rally all sectors of our society towards education for all', giving it 'highest priority at national and other levels' and 'ensuring that a growing share of national and community resources is dedicated to basic education'. The conference was organised by three United Nations agencies: the Children's Fund (UNICEF), the Educational, Scientific and Cultural Organization (UNESCO) and the Population Fund (UNFPA).

The above is an extract from *International Dateline*.

Third world population growth

Third world population growth is maintaining its record breaking pace, according to the 1994 *World Population Data Sheet*, issued by the Washington-based Population Reference Bureau (PRB). Each year, says PRB, an additional 90 million people tenant the earth, with 97 out of every 100 of these born in the developing world. Breaking this down further, PRB says that for every 1000 people now alive on our planet, 25 infants are born each year and 9 people die, leading to a 1.6% rate of natural increase for the whole population. Of the current world population of 5.6 billion, industrialised countries contain 1.2 billion people while developing countries are home to 4.4 billion. According to PRB, women in the richer countries average about 1.7 children each during their lifetime while in developing countries, the average is 3.6. When China is excluded from the calculations, developing country women average 4.2 children each. Population growth rates are still on the upswing in developing countries despite the growing number of public and private family planning services available, says PRB. The rapid growth rate is particularly evident in Africa where each woman gives birth to an average of 5 to 8 children. If the current growth rate of 2.9 percent continues, PRB says, Africa will double its population every 24 years. Although family planning programs showed early success in Africa, says PRB, the long term effect is unknown. Demographers Carl Haub and Machiko Yanagishita, authors of the *Data Sheet*, concluded that: 'While it appears that increased emphasis on population problems may yet stem the tide, prospects for population growth in the Third World remain essentially unchanged.'

Global trends

The growth in human numbers which lies ahead is the fastest in history. The global total of 5.6 billion in 1994 may top 10 billion during the lifetime of today's 20-year-olds and could reach 28 billion by the year 2150

However, if governments give high priority to fulfilling the unmet demand for family planning and to improving women's status, female education and maternal and child health care, world population may not exceed nine billion.

The first two billion
For most of prehistory human numbers grew very slowly, reaching approximately five million in 5000 BC. The Agricultural Revolution permitted much faster growth and world population increased to 300 million at the time of Jesus. It took until 1804 to reach the first billion.

The Industrial Revolution allowed a further population increase and the growth rate accelerated to about 0.6 per cent a year. The second billion was reached in 1928 – only 124 years after the first.

Rapid growth since 1940
It was a radical improvement in health care from 1950 onwards that brought rapid rates of population growth. Antibiotics, vaccination and spraying against malaria caused a drop in death rates. Birth rates fell much more slowly. This gap between death rates and birth rates led to sudden population growth.

The third human billion was reached only 32 years after the second, in 1960. World population reached its peak growth rate of 2.1 per cent a year in the years 1965–70, and the fourth billion was added in only 14 years. The fifth, reached in 1987, took a mere 13 years.

The explosion ahead
The *rate* of growth has since slowed down and is now around 1.6 per cent a year. But the annual increase in numbers is still growing.

We are on the threshold of the peak years: 1995–2000. Over this period, according to the United Nations medium projection, 94 million extra humans will be added annually for another two decades. This is equal to six Netherlands every year; an extra UK, France or Italy every seven months; the whole of Europe, East and West, in just over five years.

Alternative futures
United Nations medium projections have a very good record of accuracy over the past 30 years. If that record continues, we can expect a world population of about 8.5 billion by 2025 – an extra 2.9 billion on top of today's. The total would rise to just over 10 billion by 2050, levelling off at 11.5 billion by 2150.

The medium projection assumes that past progress in bringing down birth rates is maintained. But if we continue to make poor progress in the crucial decades ahead, we could be on target for the UN high projection. This would mean a world population of 9.4 billion people by 2025 and 12.5 billion by 2050.

What happens after 2050 depends on varying assumptions about women's fertility – the number of children they have in their lifetime. If they had just enough children to replace themselves (about 2.1), world population would level off at around 11.5 billion by 2150. If women went on having 2.2 to 2.5 children each, we could be heading for a world population of 21 to 28 billion by 2150.

Aiming low – the safe option
But less crowded futures are possible. If all developing countries' fertility rates decreased as fast as countries like Thailand, South Korea or Sri Lanka, then we could be on line for the UN's low projection. In that case world population would peak at 7.8 billion in 2050. This is 2.2 billion less than the medium projection, and a massive 4.7 billion less than the high.

After 2050 the low projection assumes that women all over the world will follow the pattern of today's European countries and have only 1.7 children each. If this happens, after 2050 world population would start to decline. By 2150 it could be back down to today's level.

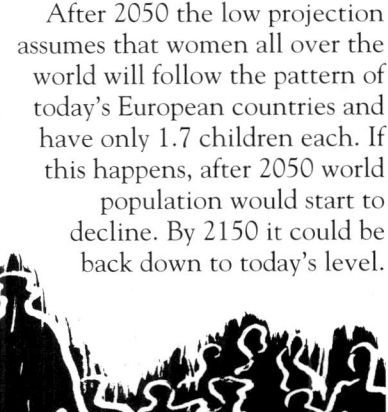

The shifting balance

Over the next three decades the balance of world population will shift dramatically. In developed countries population growth has slowed to less than 0.6 per cent a year. In Europe it is less than half of that: populations in most European countries will probably start to decline after 2005.

Future growth will be heavily concentrated in the South. Some 94 per cent of increases between 1995 and 2025 will occur in developing countries. Their populations are expected to rise by almost two thirds, from about 4.4 billion now to 7.1 billion.

This will mean massive shifts in the geo-political balance. In 1950 today's developed countries made up one third of the world's population. By 2025 they will dwindle to only 17 per cent. By 2050 on the medium projection, Africa's population may have trebled to 2.27 billion, from about 740 million in 1995. These changes will inevitably increase the pressures for migration from South to North.

A crowded future

The prospects for some countries are daunting. According to World Bank demographers, Nigeria's population may rise from its current 100 million to an eventual 382 million before

There is an alternative. The growth in human numbers could be slowed through the uptake of voluntary family planning

stabilising towards 2100. Tanzania's numbers could increase five-fold from about 25 million now to 116 million.

The challenges will not be confined to Africa. Arab countries will see their numbers multiply almost as quickly as Africa's. Syria's population may quintuple from 13 million now to 69 million, Iran's could rise from 60 million to 354 million. Pakistan's could grow from 120 million to 402 million.

India's population could more than double from 914 million in 1994 to an eventual 1.89 billion. With its present population of 125 million, Bangladesh is already twice as densely populated as the Netherlands. Yet the country may have to accommodate 268 million people.

Uncertainties and options

All these projections are based on expected trends in fertility and mortality. It is conceivable that some of the totals may never be reached because environmental changes, or shortages of key natural resources like land and water may impose limits.

The AIDS epidemic is another imponderable. Some people have speculated that AIDS might offer an apocalyptic 'solution' to the world population problem. This argument is offensive and probably incorrect. Present studies suggest that AIDS might reduce populations in only a few countries. Elsewhere it will merely slow growth a little.

There is an alternative. The growth in human numbers could be slowed through the uptake of voluntary family planning. There is a high level of unmet need for family planning. Merely satisfying the demand by providing family planning to women and men who would like to use contraception but lack the means and opportunity to do so, would ensure that the world remained on target for the medium projection and did not exceed 11.5 billion.

Even faster progress could be made if the demand for family planning increased further. Investing in female education, improving women's status and reducing infant mortality through mother and child health care are all contributory factors. If governments in the South gave these matters a higher priority, and governments in the North helped them to do so, the world's population could remain below nine billion.

Bibliography

Individual country long range projections from World Bank, *World Development Report 1993*, World Bank, Washington DC, 1993; McEvedy, C. and Jones, R., *Atlas of World Population History*, Penguin, 1978; United Nations Population Division, *Long Range World Population Projections*, United Nations, New York, 1992; United Nations Population Division, *World Population Prospects 1992*, United Nations, New York, 1993.

● The above is an extract from *Briefing Pack – on Population and Development*. See page 39 for address details.

© *Maries Stopes International*

Photo: IPPF / Jeremy Hamand

There is a high level of unmet need for family planning

Tax parenthood to save the world

Liz Hunt reports on radical proposals from a top British surgeon to help control the growing global population

Couples should have to apply for a licence to have children and there should be a tax penalty for parents who have more than two offspring, according to proposals on population control by a leading surgeon, himself a father of six.

Professor Sir Roy Calne, 64, a world-renowned transplant surgeon and leading figure of the British medical establishment, also discusses the creation of a virus – 'the 'O' virus, a hypothetical fertility limiter' – in a controversial book out this month.

Other disincentives to procreation include an age limit on parenting and compulsory 'pre-parenting' counselling, which begins at school.

Professor Calne is contrite about his own contribution to the population explosion and says that if he was marrying today, he would not be planning a family of six. But it is no longer reasonable to reproduce when the 'whim' takes you, he explains, adding that he loves all his children. 'They are grown up now and gainfully employed; they are not a drain on the state.'

Too many people are draining both the 'global' state and the planet, says Professor Calne, who has saved hundreds of lives in his career. He makes no apology for his views. 'We are on a disaster course. World population stands at 5 billion. There is not much time left. This is the reason I have had the audacity to examine these matters,' he said yesterday. Mass migration and worldwide conflict are the most likely outcome if governments fail to act, he believes.

His book, *Too Many People*, was prompted in part by a visit to Bombay and by the debate surrounding his own speciality, transplant surgery, where costly high tech medicine is needed to save a single life. Professor Calne pioneered transplantation for children at Addenbrooke's Hospital in Cambridge, and in March completed the first six organ transplant in Britain.

'The book was really precipitated by people saying transplantation was a waste of money; why should we spend so much money on a few people when there are so many terrible things happening in the world?' said Professor Calne. 'I was thinking about this when I was in Bombay where 1 million people around the airport are in the most dreadful poverty and this prompted me to start writing about it.

'There are so many interacting facets it became quite difficult – religion, human nature, politics, economics and the biology of reproduction and contraception. I homed in on what I do know about and my main thesis, though not particularly original, is that most of our troubles are due to scientific advances and the use of science without really knowing where it's going to go.'

Radical forms of birth control may be the only answer, he argues in the book, which carries a foreword by his close friend, Terry Waite. He proposes a population control laboratory where the world's experts would resolve the problems man has created for himself. The laboratory should be situated in Delhi, Cairo or Rio, 'somewhere that those coming to work each day would be reminded of the problems', Calne said.

The aim of his book is to inform the layman and persuade politicians to act now. 'It is a serious attempt to warn the average man that the application of science has radically changed the relationship of man to other creatures,' he said.

'My proposed solution is to use the highly successful scientific method applied to each and all of the subjects discussed to try and reconcile our new knowledge with the rest of the world.'

And despite his doubts of the value of his own work on a global scale, it is not something he will be giving up. 'On a personal and professional level, I see myself with my Hippocratic hat on; you do your best for your patient regardless of whether you like them or their lifestyle. As a citizen of the world, I wear a more "fearful" hat.'

© *The Independent*
August, 1994

Population and fertility rates

There are two sorts of alarmist stories concerning birthrates. The first focus on a 'population explosion', with high birthrates being blamed for poverty, famine and other problems. The second warn of a 'birth dearth', with populations having so few children that they are unable even to replace themselves. The concerns here are different, focussing on 'race suicide', the lack of vitality and entrepreneurial risk-taking skills in an ageing workforce, and the problem of paying for pensions and health care for a large elderly population, when the younger, working-age population is shrinking.

The 'population explosion' is associated with the developing countries; the 'birth dearth' with the rich countries. In reality, there has been such a dramatic drop in fertility worldwide within the last generation that the prospect of a 'population explosion' seems scarcely realistic.

Total Period Fertility Rate

The Total Period Fertility Rate (TPFR) tells us the average completed family size at a given time. In order for the population to replace itself, women in developed countries need to have an average of 2.1 children – 2 to replace the woman and her partner, and the 0.1 to cover people who, for various reasons, do not reproduce.

In developing countries the replacement level of fertility will be higher, owing to higher rates of mortality, especially infant mortality. In other words, women need to have more children to ensure that a sufficient number grow to adulthood and reproduce to replace their parents' generation.

Table 1 shows that fertility rates have fallen dramatically throughout the world since 1975, in both the developed and the developing countries.

There are still very large differences between rich and poor countries. For example, it is still usual in many African countries for women to have an average of six children or more, while in the European Union the TPFR is below replacement level for every country except Ireland. However, the worldwide trend is down, in all continents.

Europe

In Europe nearly all countries are significantly below replacement level. The French and the British have fertility rates which have been stable at around 1.8 for more than ten years. In Italy – a country reputed to love children – the TPFR is 1.25 children per woman. This is the lowest in the world. In Eastern Europe some countries have tried to raise the birthrate, with limlted success.

Africa

The African birthrate remains high, but with urbanisation and modernisation proceeding, it is estimated that there may be a substantial drop. Nigeria, the most populous country in Africa with nearly 90 million people, has an estimated TPFR of 6.9 children. Whilst fertility rates are higher in Africa, so is replacement level owing to high rates of mortality. The replacement level would probably be about 2.8 children per woman, rather than 2.1. Because Africa only accounts for about 12% of the world population the high birthrate has little impact on global trends.

America – USA and Canada

The North American birthrate has been rising in recent years, and appears to have now reached replacement level of 2.1. In the USA and Canada there is a tradition of early marriage and higher fertility than in Europe. The influence of the USA through TV and films on world culture makes it an important

Table 1: United Nations estimates of total fertility rates and percentage change: World and Major Areas 1975-80, 1980-85 and 1985-1990					
	Total fertility rate			Percentage change	
major area and region	1975-80	1980-85	1985-90	1975-80 1980-85	1980-85 1985-90
World	3.84	3.60	3.45	-6.3	-4.2
More developed regions	3.03	1.93	1.89	-4.9	-2.1
Less developed regions	4.54	4.19	3.94	-7.7	-6.0
Least developed countries	6.63	6.38	6.16	-3.8	-3.4

indicator of world trends in some respects, but there is as yet no sign that other countries in the Western world are following the USA towards replacement fertility.

America – Latin America and the Caribbean

Here there have been steep falls in fertility rates. The two most populous countries are Brazil (150 million people) and Mexico (90 million people). Between the early 1970s and 1985/6 the TPFR in Mexico fell from 6.1 to 3.8 children per woman, and in Brazil from 5.7 to 3.0.

Australasia

The pattern is similar to that for Europe and most other developed nations, with fertility rates below replacement level. The population is too small to influence world trends.

Asia

The majority of the world's people live in Asia (3.1 billion out of a total of 5.3 billion in 1990). Population trends in Asia therefore largely determine global trends. Some Asian countries, like Japan and South Korea, have highly developed industrial economies and tend to imitate Western patterns of below replacement fertility. The TPFR in Hong Kong fell from 2.7 in the mid-1970s to 1.4 in the mid 1980s – the lowest in Asia.

However, it is in the large Asian countries, especially in China (1990 pop. 1.2 billion) and India (1991 pop. 843 million), which between them account for more than a third of the world's population, that the steep fall in fertility rates in recent years is most apparent. This is partly owing to the strong preference for sons in these countries, which has led to the widespread use of ultrasonic scanning equipment to detect the sex of unborn babies, with a view to aborting females. The fertility rate (TPFR) which is required to achieve replacement level of the population is affected by the ratio of males to females in the population. If steps are taken which interfere with the natural balance of males and females in live births, this alters the level of fertility needed to replace the population.

	Fertility (TPFR)	Replacement level	Percentage of replacement fertility being achieved
UK	1.8	2.1	76%
Ireland	2.4	2.1	114%
Italy	1.25	2.1	60%
China	1.6	2.8	57%
India	4.0	2.4	167%
Uganda	7.0	2.7	259%
USA	2.0	2.1	95%

Table 2: Approximate levels of fertility and replacement fertility in various countries, circa 1991.

China's missing million

The shortage of female births is at its most extreme in China which operates the world's largest and most coercive population programme – the famous one-child-per-couple policy. This has led to a resurgence of the traditional Chinese practice of female infanticide, as 'son preference' is very strong in Chinese culture. Many parents are unwilling to accept a daughter as an only child. The shortfall of female births is so extreme that the ratio of male/female births has been estimated at 1.6 to 1.0, and it appears that birth statistics are a million females 'light' each year. Taking into account Chinese levels of mortality and infant mortality, which are good by the standards of developing countries, this gives a replacement fertility level of 2.8 children per woman.

The one-child policy is more strictly enforced in the towns (where the TPFR is given as 1.5) than in the countryside (where it is 2.8). Speaking at the London School of Economics in November 1993, Dr X-Z Peng, Director of Population Studies in Shanghai University, said that the one child policy should really be called the 1.6 child policy, as he believed this to be the true TPFR. (It had been 5.4 in 1971 – an unprecedented drop.) This means that fertility levels in China are running at only 57% of what is required to replace the population – a more extreme shortfall than anything experienced by Western European nations. The demographic problems facing China will soon be more like those associated with the 'birth dearth' than the 'population explosion'.

• The above is from *Population Information Pack* published by the Committee on Population and the Economy. See page 39 for address details.

© *Committee on Population*

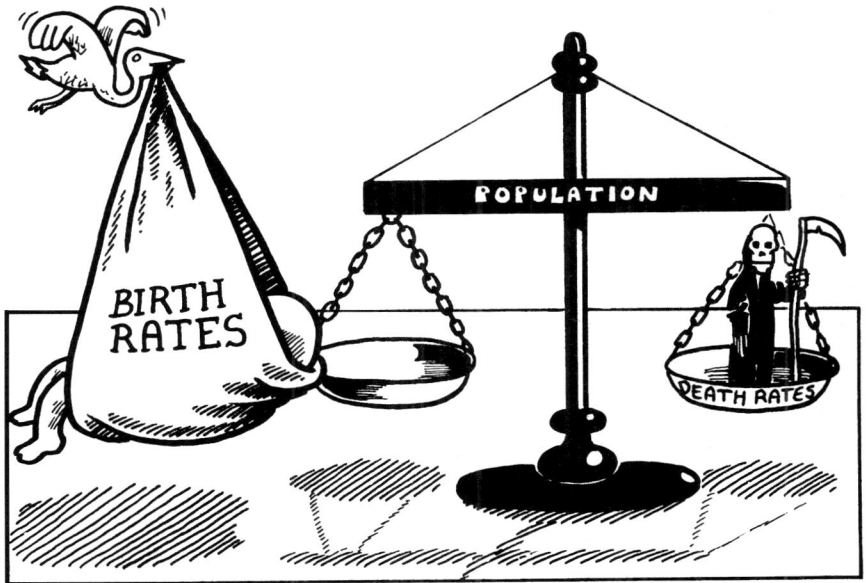

Population myths

It is easy to panic about population growth. All kinds of confusing images from newspapers, television and charity adverts get mixed together: millions of starving people, a planet overburdened, population in the billions and still rising, a world incapable of sustaining all its people.

Such vague images can help form beliefs about the population explosion that are no more than a thinly veiled racism: fear and prejudice combine to fuel discrimination against and hatred of black and Asian people. There is also a dangerous climate of opinion that suggests the solutions are easy. What is important is to see this whole issue in context, at both country and community level.

This article untangles these confusions. It sets out of the most common misconceptions about population, and explains clearly the true situation and Save the Children's position. Putting the facts, and explaining the context, doesn't remove the problems – but it does make them manageable. It makes it possible to see where to start, how to prioritise, and most of all, to work with others to tackle the issues in a way that will succeed.

This short article is an extract from a series which began with the highly-acclaimed *Famine Myths*, first published by Save the Children in 1991. For copies of both booklets see the address on page 39.

Myth 1

Population growth is the biggest single problem facing the world today.

It is not. Population growth is a big problem. But it is a symptom of other problems, such as poverty, high death rates of children, and inadequate access to food. There is clearly a link between economic security and the decision to limit family size. In other words, when people know that they and their family can be properly provided for, they may have fewer children. There is little evidence that it works the other way.

THE PROBLEM IN THE THIRD WORLD IS THAT THEY BREED LIKE FLIES!

Ken Pyne

That means it is a wasted effort to try to tackle population head on by urging people to have smaller families. Such single-minded approaches will quite simply fail. The best and most successful initiatives tackle underlying causes too – by finding ways of reducing poverty and insecurity and improving mother and child health. For example in the slums of Khulna, Bangladesh, Save the Children supports a network of community volunteers who mobilise women to start self-help projects – generating income from cottage industries like sewing. Community health workers also promote family spacing and safe childbirth methods to traditional midwives. This integrated approach is clearly working: both fertility rates and infant mortality have dropped. Families are working together to solve other problems like overcrowding, drainage, poor water and sanitation.

- The rate of population growth worldwide is not rising. It has been the same since about 1975, about 1.7% a year.

- Fertility is actually falling. It is calculated as 3.8 per woman from 1975 to 1980 and 3.3 per woman between 1990 and 1995.

- The number of people added to the population each year is rising rapidly, because of past growth. In 1975 the annual addition was about 72 million. In 1992 it was 93 million. It will peak between 1995 and 2000 at about 98 million a year.

- The population worldwide in mid-1994 was 5.66 billion. It is projected to increase to 6.25 billion by 2000, 8.5 billion in 2025 and 10 billion in 2050

- In the industrialised countries of Europe and North America, population growth has slowed or stopped entirely. Fertility rates are at or below the level needed to replace the population.
  Source: The State of World Population 1993 and 1994, United Nations Population Fund

Note: the total fertility rate is a way of comparing the numbers of children born to women in different parts the world and at different periods.

Myth 2

People have too many babies because they do not know any better.

On the contrary, people have babies for very precise and sensible reasons. In certain circumstances, in certain parts of the world, having a large family is the logical option. Imagine that there is no health service, no welfare benefits, no pension scheme, no provision at all for when you get old or sick and can no longer work. In this case 'social security' is your family. A large family can bring security and hope for the future. A small family is risky and makes you dependent on outside help.

It is easy to imagine the effects of high infant mortality on birth rates: in Niger, Angola, Mozambique and Afghanistan, for example, more than one in four children die before they reach the age of five. Low wages can push up the birth rate too – you need more hands to bring in a living wage for a family. In these circumstances, it might be said that to have a small family is to act irresponsibly.

A number of complex factors will determine family size, including the economic climate, migration patterns, access to education, religious beliefs, the status of women in society, the chances of children surviving and the age and sex structure of the population. This makes it difficult to generalise: what seems to be true of one country will quite definitely not be true of another.

And, of course, there are people who do not have proper access to contraception advice and services in all parts of the world. They would like to limit family size but have no means of getting contraceptives. Save the Children supports government efforts to provide such services, as part of an overall package of health services which are a basic right.

Some people mistakenly believe that the so-called street children of the world's growing cities are all orphans or abandoned and unwanted children. They are not. Most are doing casual and dangerous work to bring much-needed income to their families. The work is poorly paid, precarious and sometimes illegal, but it is the only way they can contribute to the family income.

- For example, Alvin, 11, spends most of his time on the streets of Montego Bay, Jamaica, where he collects and sells empty bottles, does odd jobs, begs and at times has to steal to support himself and his mother. 'Alvin makes sure that whatever he hustles is shared between himself and his mother,' says Glenda Drummond, project worker at a Save the Children project for street children, which has helped Alvin return to school.
- In Ho Chi Minh City, Vietnam, 15-year-old Loan works on the railway station selling fans to passengers for half a dollar a day at most. She, too, had to drop out of school. She eats at a drop-in centre for street children but sleeps at her father's home.

Myth 3

We must tackle population growth – if necessary by force – before we can solve other world problems.

Beyond the moral arguments, this approach cannot work in the long run without heavy social costs – such as female infanticide. What kind of world would it be where some people had the right to reproduce and others did not? Save the Children believes that it is the absolute and unconditional right of individual women and men to decide the size of their family. Any form of bribery, rewards or incentives to promote contraception or sterilisation is wrong in principle and ineffective in practice.

Population growth is not some separate problem that just happens through ignorance or wilful irresponsibility. There are precise reasons for it and Save the Children is dedicated to tackling them holistically, as part of a whole development programme, as well as trying to understand why people act as they do. The only way to limit population growth on a lasting basis is to create the conditions in which women have the power to choose smaller families. What this means in practice will vary from country to country, according to the particular needs of the community. All useful interventions are likely to fall into one or more of the following interrelated categories:

Promoting economic development

Boosting the economic security of the world's poorest people is a vital part of the process of reducing family size. Many factors have to be considered when assessing strategies: as well as fertility and mortality, migration patterns are a very significant, and growing, influence on population trends.

Poverty limits people's choices. So Save the Children works at local level to increase people's economic security. It supports income generation projects, especially for women, alongside services which save time and labour – such as clean water supplied close to home, and nutrition and women's education projects.

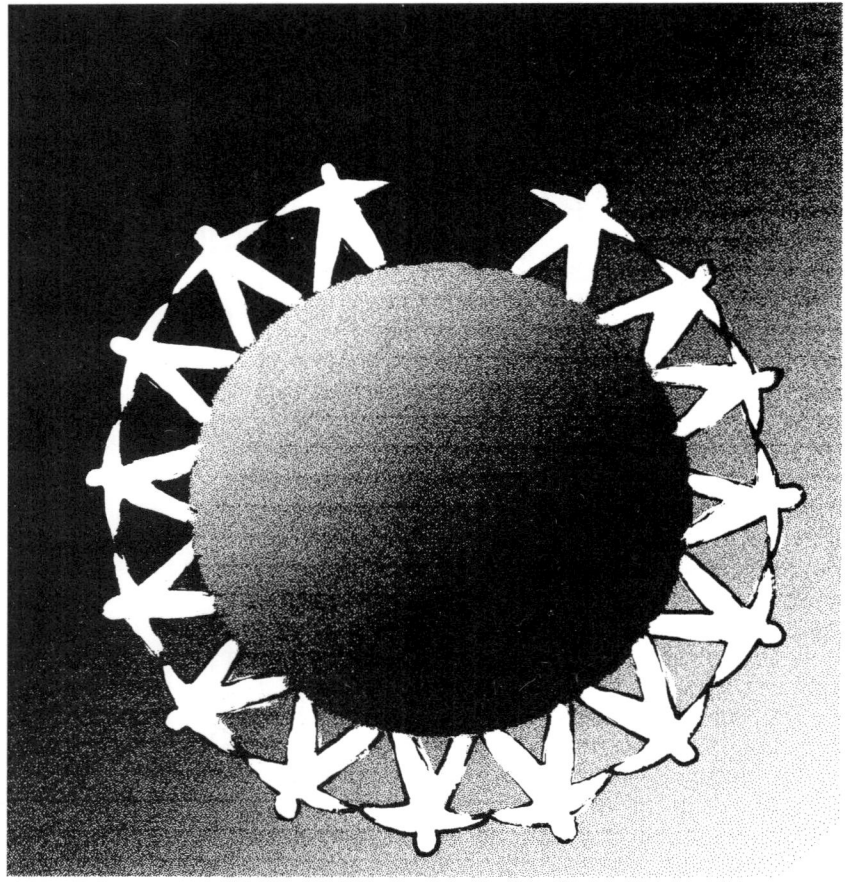

Reducing child deaths

Once people know that their children are more likely to survive, their confidence grows. The security they and their families need can come from fewer children – so the birth rate falls. Better health care and preventive action is vital, with services specifically targeted at mothers and children.

Raising women's status, health and education

Good health and adequate nutrition are vital to women's own survival and well-being, as well as those of their children. They are also linked to falling birth rates, as are improvements in women's standing in society, their literacy, access to education and their ability to generate income.

Obviously these improve the quality of life for women and their families; they are also one of the most effective ways of reducing population growth.

Providing family planning services

There is no perfect method of birth control. The secret of successful programmes is to offer people a choice of affordable methods that are appropriate to their life-style, needs and beliefs. Save the Children particularly stresses the value of breast-feeding as a natural method of child spacing.

Most importantly, the contraceptive methods offered must be consistently available and part of a wider health service, provided by health workers trained in family planning and counselling.

Access to education for girls and women is critical to reducing high fertility rates. Studies show that, on average, women with seven or more years' education marry more than five years later than women without any education and have two to three fewer children. Secondary school enrolment is low for women: 48% in Latin America and the Caribbean, 28% in South Asia, and 14% in sub-Saharan Africa.

Myth 4

No wonder there is famine in the Third World – there are just too many mouths to feed.

Famine is not caused by over-population. It is caused by poverty.

In famines people suffer because they have no access to food – not because there is not enough of it to go around.

In any case, incidence of famine simply does not match up with areas of high population. Much of Africa is, in fact, very sparsely populated. There are many more mouths to feed per square kilometre in Holland than anywhere else in the world. But when did the Dutch last face famine?

Many people worry that somehow the world's resources, including food stocks, are being depleted by large populations in the Third World. They feel that we might run out of food. This is not true or fair. We produce enough food for everyone on the planet. And we can continue to do so for populations much larger than even the greatest predictions. It is the way that food is shared out that is the problem.

Do not forget, too, that the Northern industrialised countries consume, waste and destroy immeasurably more per person than those in the South. You might as well say, no wonder there is famine in the Third World, there are just too many overfed, wasteful, destructive people in the First World.

● Are we running short of food? Global food production, of food grain alone, is around two billion tons a year. Four people can reasonably exist on a ton a year (and that is more than many people in the developing world currently get). So today we produce enough to feed eight billion people. In other words, we could already feed our current population, plus another 30%. We also have the technology to achieve a dramatic increase in food supply in many countries.

Source: Seaman, John. *Population, food supply, and famine: an ecological or an economic dilemma?* in Sir Bryan Cartledge (ed.), Health and the Environment, Oxford University Press, October 1994.

● The above is an extract from *Population Myths*, a free booklet available from Save the Children. See page 39 for address details.

The three culprits

Population, consumption, technology

A furious controversy is raging over the link between population growth and problems in the environment. Some people say population growth is the number one culprit. Others blame consumption in the rich countries. Others again single out technology.

They can't all be right. Or can they? When you think about it logically, every one of us – from the poor African farmer to the company director – is a consumer. How much damage we do to the environment depends on how much each one of us consumes.

A lot depends, too, on how efficient our technology is: how many resources are used to meet our consumer needs, and how much waste is produced. If I ride 10 miles on a bike, I use no resources and emit no pollutants. If I drive the same distance in a car I burn petrol, create air pollution, and add to global warming. Tech-nology is always a factor –from the hunter gatherer with a harpoon, to the fishing boat with a three-mile drift net.

Population becomes important when we're trying to work out the total damage that our country, or the human race, is doing. The more people consuming at a certain level, the more damage they will do.

These three factors, population, consumption per person, and technology, are all important. They are never, ever, found apart. The damage done is the effect of all three working together. The damage at present is vast, because we have never been so numerous before. We have never consumed so much before. And we have never used such damaging technologies before.

If we are looking at the increase in damage, then at different times and places, different factors may be more important. In Africa and Asia, the main cause of deforestation is the growth of population.

Illustration: Greg Spalenka / Image Bank

Technology was the key agent in opening the ozone hole. The direct cause was chlorofluorocarbons (CFCs) – used in fridges, hair sprays, foam packing and so on. These chemicals were not commercialised till 1928. Their use rocketed in the West from the 1940s on, and this had very little to do with population growth. Sometimes growing consumption is the chief culprit – as with air pollution in Europe. However, technology changes here have tended to improve things. Factory chimneys have filters. More and more cars have catalytic converters to clean exhaust gases. And the population is growing only slowly.

Our three culprits are the ones that do direct harm to our environment. But of course, there are many other factors which work through these three. Poverty, for example, pushes people to have more children as social security for old age. Inequality is important. In Latin America or South Africa a few big landowners corner most of the land. The landless are cramped into dry, hilly or forest areas, which they are forced to overuse and destroy.

Democracy and free markets matter, too. Where free speech and free elections are allowed, people can protest against pollution, and pollution can be cut. If prices are free and firms can keep profits, they have an incentive to use resources carefully; the Communist economies tended to waste energy and minerals, and pollu-tion remained high.

We can't single out one suspect. If we do, the others will go scot free – and the damage will continue.

● The above is an extract from the *Moving Pictures Bulletin*, a special issue on Population, produced jointly by Central Television and Television Trust for the Environment (TVE). See page 39 for address details.

© TVE & Central Television
February, 1995

The three impacts

Depleting resources, production of wastes, the need for more space

The earth is our habitat. Like all animals, we use it in three main ways. Firstly, as a source of resources such as food, building materials and energy. Some resources, such as energy from the sun, or trees, or fish, are renewable. Others, like oil or copper, are non-renewable – they run down as we use them.

Secondly, the land, waters and air are a sink for our wastes – not just solids, but liquids and gases. And not only what we deliberately throw away, but by-products like exhaust fumes, soil washed off farm land, or trees burned after cutting.

Last but not least, we take up space for our farms and houses, our roads and factories. That space is occupied by us, our crops, livestock and pets – so there is less room for other species. In coming years we will take up a great deal of extra space, and we can only get it at the expense of wildlife. If our numbers grow to 11.5 billion, we will need an extra 12.5 million square kilometres for our farms and cities. This is almost double the total area of all protected natural areas in the world today.

Natural resources, like food, forests or fish, are the most vulnerable

People used to worry about running out of non-renewable resources. Yet these have posed the fewest problems of all. Mineral reserves have been a magic mountain: the more we used, the more there were. World aluminium reserves in 1950 were enough to last for 30 years. But by 1980 the reserves were 3.7 times bigger than in 1950. The secret was that wider exploration found more supplies, and better techniques made lower grades of ore usable. If one resource runs out, we can always use substitutes. Solar energy is almost infinite.

Natural resources, like food, forests or fish, are the most vulnerable. Until 1985, food supplies grew in pace with population growth. But in the last seven years they have not done so. It is too early to say whether this is more than a short-term problem.

According to the United Nations Food and Agriculture Organisation, the Third World could feed as many as 33 billion people from its own lands. But to grow this much, most rainforests would have to be cut down, and massive doses of fertilisers applied.

Many countries would still face problems. In Africa, 29 countries could not feed their populations at the end of this decade using basic farming techniques. And we cannot foresee the long term effects of erosion, which is removing fertile topsoil all over the world. Almost 20 million square kilometres – an area the size of Latin America – has been degraded since 1945.

The worst problems stem from our wastes. In many cases we have already passed the limits that the atmosphere and oceans can absorb. Our waste liquids are polluting rivers and coastal seas. Increasing amounts of fertiliser are washing off farm land, and population growth is the main driving force behind the increase.

Photo: Howard J. Davies/ Panos Pictures

In coming years we will take up a great deal of extra space

The biggest threat of all comes from our gaseous wastes. When we burn fossil fuels – or forests – sulphur dioxide and nitrogen oxides are produced. These turn the rain acid, which damages forests and freshwater life. Our use of CFCs has punched a hole in the ozone layer.

Population growth was not a major factor in either of these. But it will be dominant in the longest term threat we face: global warming. This is caused mainly by increased output of carbon dioxide from fuels and forests, and of methane from paddy fields and flatulent cattle. Population growth is responsible for about two-fifths of the increase in carbon dioxide output, and for more than two thirds in the case of methane.

If, as forecast, population increases to 11.5 billion by the year 2050, we will need an extra 12.5 million square kilometres of land for our farms and cities. This additional land can be compared to:
70% of South America
41% of Africa
93% of Antarctica

Wealth and waste

So numbers do count. And numbers are growing fastest by far in the poorer, Southern countries.

Yet they are not the ones who are doing most damage to the planet. People in the Northern, industrialised countries are consuming the lion's share of the Earth's resources, and pumping out the great bulk of the world's wastes.

The more we earn, the more we consume. In 1989, in real terms, the average income in the industrial countries was six and a half times higher than in developing countries. It was 13 times higher than in Africa or South Asia. With higher incomes we buy many more possessions made of scarce resources. There were 39 cars for every hundred people in developed countries in 1988. In developing countries there were only two.

Over a lifetime, the average American produces 4000 times their own bodyweight in domestic and industrial waste. This bears no comparison to the average Third World person, who produces only 150 times their own bodyweight over the same period

---

Rich countries use far more energy of all kinds – over six times more per person. With more polluting fuels the gaps are wider. We use 10 times more oil per person, 20 times more gas, 45 times more nuclear energy.

And the more we consume, the more we waste. The average Third World person produces, over their lifetimes, 150 times their bodyweight in domestic and industrial waste. But the typical European leaves a monument 1000 times bigger than their own weight, and the average American 4000 times. At least, most of this solid waste is disposed of in the country where it is created.

But our invisible wastes are even greater, and they flood out into the great global commons, the atmosphere and the oceans. Every year, every person in an industrialised country pumps out a balloon of carbon dioxide weighing eleven and a half tonnes into the atmosphere – 177 times their own bodyweight. The average person in a developing country produces only one ninth as much.

Developed countries pump out three quarters of the carbon dioxide that stokes global warming, and seven eighths of the CFCs that destroy the ozone layer.

In terms of how much damage each person does, the gaps are wider still. Everyone in a rich country accounts for five and a half times more fertilizer washed into the sea, and 75 times more poisonous waste, than the average person from a poorer country.

So we need to be concerned about population growth in the North, as well as in the South. Northern populations are growing slowly, but they are still growing. The 57 million people who will be added to their numbers during the 1990s could do as much damage to the earth's atmosphere and oceans as the 911 million extra people in the South.

Parents in rich countries should think hard before condemning the average Indian who has four or five children, or the African who has six or seven children. The truth is that a 'small' Western family with only two children has as much impact on the globe as one with 40 children in Africa or India.

● The above is an extract from the *Moving Pictures Bulletin*, a special issue on Population, produced jointly by Central Television and Television Trust for the Environment (TVE). See page 39 for address details.

© TVE & Central Television February, 1995

Population

Resources and the environment

Two centuries of debate

The link between population growth and environmental damage is one of the most controversial development issues. The debate began in earnest back in 1798, with the publication of Thomas Malthus' *Essay on Population*. Malthus believed that food supply could never grow as fast as population i.e. food supply grows arithmetically (1, 2, 3, 4 . . .) whilst population grows geometrically (1, 2, 4, 8, 16 . . .). Ultimately, he argued, the increase in human numbers would also be kept in check by famine, 'the most dreadful resource of nature'.

Paul Ehrlich, in his 1968 book *The Population Bomb*, restated Malthus' views in modern form. Sometime between 1970 and 1985, he predicted there would be vast famines in which hundreds of millions of people would starve to death. The Club of Rome's 1972 computer-projected study, *The Limits to Growth*, threatened catastrophic resource shortages and pollution leading to a population collapse in the second half of the next century. Performed again in 1992, their follow-up study, *Beyond the Limits*, showed that population, consumption and technology had already surpassed the earth's limits. Only a drastic slowdown in population growth, coupled with recycling, better crop yields, soil conservation and pollution control, could avert this disaster.

But the picture is not all rosy. World cereal production per person peaked in 1986 and is lower now than at any time since 1975

Such alarmist statements have brought forth strong opposition. US economist Julian Simon argued in *The Ultimate Resource* in 1981 that population growth had been a boon – the extra brainpower brings solutions to any problems that might arise. Resources had not grown scarcer, as Malthusians predicted, but more abundant. United Nations researcher Ester Boserup claimed that rising population density was essential for technological progress.

On mineral resources the anti-Malthusians have been winning the argument so far. The reserves of many minerals are larger now than in 1950 despite four decades of massive use – thanks to exploration and improved technology. Some minerals and fossil fuels will inevitably have grown scarce in the next century – but technology allows us to switch to substitutes, or economise on use.

On food too, Malthus has been proved wrong. Food production has grown, on average, faster than population. During the 1980s the fastest progress was registered by Asia, where food production per person rose by 2 per cent a year. Average intakes of calories and protein in most developing countries have also improved, partly the result of increased food imports.

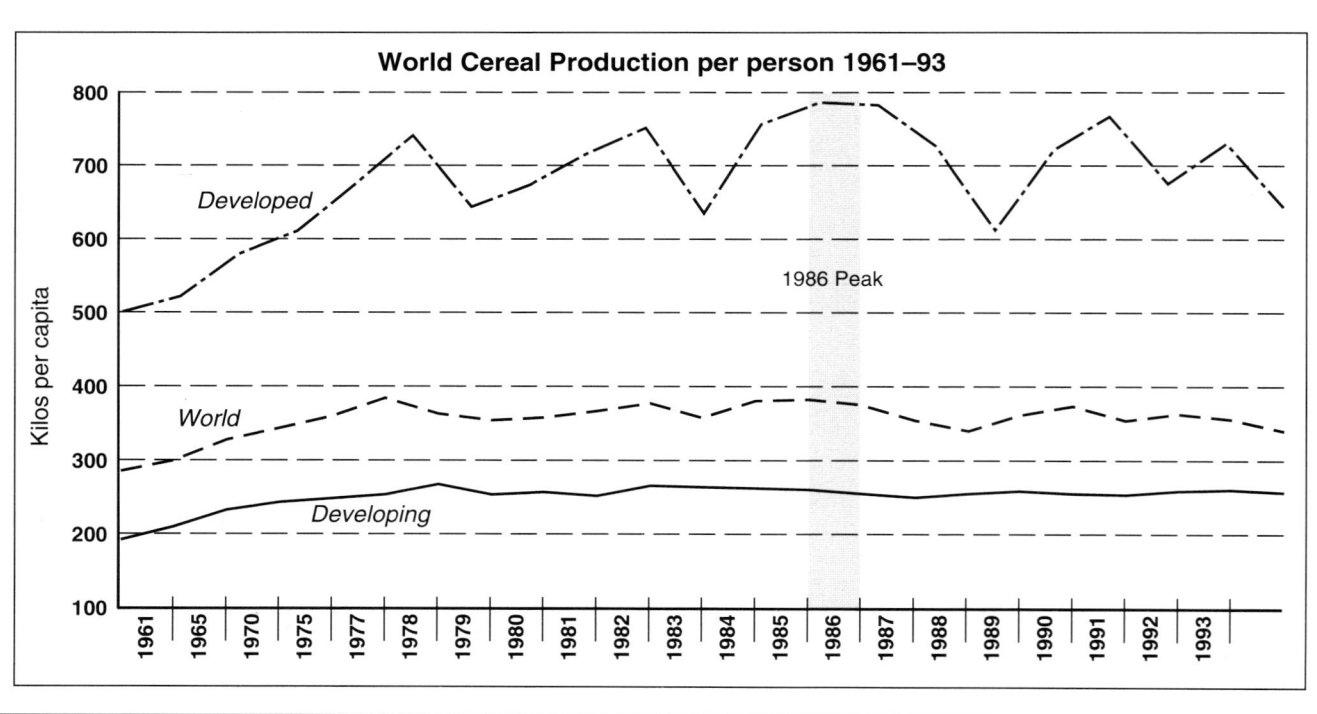

World Cereal Production per person 1961–93

But the picture is not all rosy. World cereal production per person peaked in 1986 and is lower now than at any time since 1975. In 73 out of 113 developing countries – and in 36 out of 45 countries in sub-Saharan Africa – food production failed to keep pace with population growth during the 1980s. Furthermore, during this period food consumption per person fell in 37 out of 103 developing countries.

In future we can expect this uneven pattern to continue. The world as a whole may be able to feed any probable world population up to 12 or 13 billion, yet many individual countries will face difficulties. In most of these cases the outcome will not be spectacular famine or population collapse, but the slow attrition of infant mortality and child death.

A simple equation

Devised by Paul Ehrlich and John Holdren in 1974, the simple equation below has been used to describe in very simplified terms the inter-relationships between population, consumption, technology and the environment.

$$I = P \times A \times T$$

$I = Impact$
represents the environmental impact

$P = Population$
represents population (absolute size, growth, distribution etc.)

$A = Affluence$
represents per capita consumption of that population and is determined by income and lifestyle

$T = Technology$
represents the polluting influence of the specific technology the consumption involves.

For instance, it can demonstrate quite clearly why industrialised countries (with relatively small populations) can generate a vast impact on the environment, because the A and T factors per capita are exceptionally large. Alternatively, developing countries, with large populations but limited economic development, can also be shown to

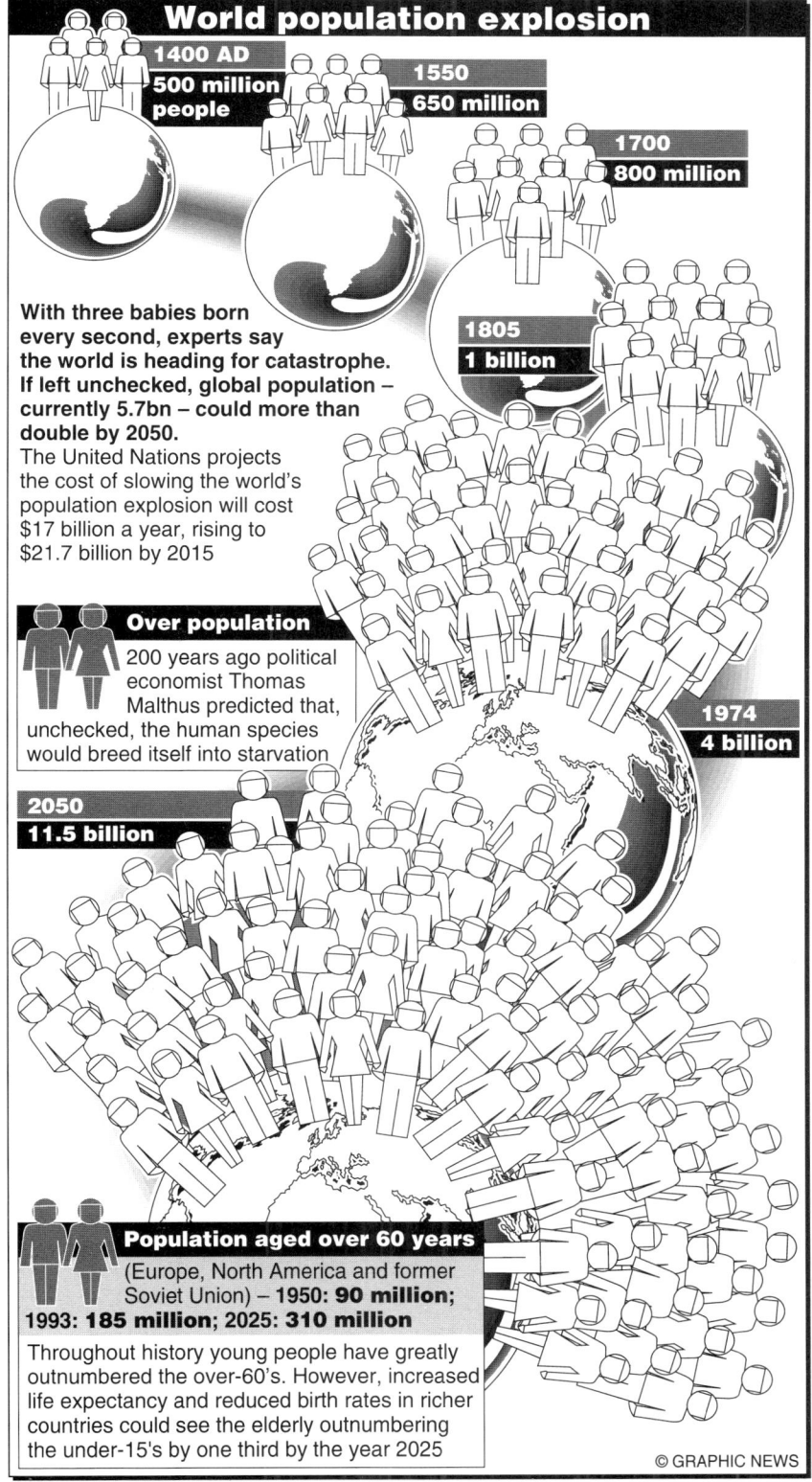

World population explosion

1400 AD
500 million people

1550
650 million

1700
800 million

1805
1 billion

1974
4 billion

2050
11.5 billion

With three babies born every second, experts say the world is heading for catastrophe. If left unchecked, global population – currently 5.7bn – could more than double by 2050.
The United Nations projects the cost of slowing the world's population explosion will cost $17 billion a year, rising to $21.7 billion by 2015

Over population
200 years ago political economist Thomas Malthus predicted that, unchecked, the human species would breed itself into starvation

Population aged over 60 years
(Europe, North America and former Soviet Union) – 1950: **90 million**; 1993: **185 million**; 2025: **310 million**
Throughout history young people have greatly outnumbered the over-60's. However, increased life expectancy and reduced birth rates in richer countries could see the elderly outnumbering the under-15's by one third by the year 2025

© GRAPHIC NEWS

have a vast impact on the environment if only because the P multiplier on A and T is so large.

However, the equation does not address the natural vulnerability of the environment itself, nor does it account for cultural, economic and institutional aspects of consumption and technology, but it does illustrate the point that the impact of an individual on the environment may seem harmless but where human numbers are substantial, the impact can be staggering.

© *Population Concern 1994*

Why population growth improves the environment

New book will help Africans to defy Western pedants

Robert Whelan, Director of the Committee on Population and the Economy, reviews *More People, Less Erosion: Environmental Recovery in Kenya* by Mary Tiffen, Michael Mortimore and Francis Gichuki, published by John Wiley and Sons, Baffins Lane, Chichester, West Sussex PO19 1UD. Price £22.50 plus £3.00 pp.

One by one, the arguments for population control have been collapsing. There is now ample evidence to show that population growth does not cause poverty or famine, and it certainly has not led to the exhaustion of natural resources predicted by such doom-mongers as the authors of the Club of Rome report *The Limits to Growth*.

Those who advocate population control programmes have come to rely almost exclusively on the environmental arguments.

'Yes,' they say, 'human beings are inventive. They can get richer even as their numbers increase, but at what a cost to the planet! We are destroying the very natural resource base we depend upon so that soon (fill in your own date here) the earth will become so polluted it will not support us.'

More People, Less Erosion is a very remarkable book which drives a coach and horses through the assumptions which underpin this scary scenario. The authors have made a detailed study of the Machakos District in Kenya from 1930 to 1989. During that time the population has increased by more than five times, and some parts of the district have a population density of 400 people per square kilometre, which is extremely high. However, food output has increased by more than three times per head of population, and by more than ten times per acre.

Most significantly, however, the environment has been improved and not degraded by this increase in human beings and their activities. Environmental problems which suggested irreversible degradation to colonial administrators in the 1930s have been dealt with, not in spite of but because of population growth.

Problem

For example, the major environmental problem which was observed at the beginning of the period under review was the loss of topsoil as a result of heavy rains following prolonged dry spells. This was dealt with by the terracing of the hillsides – a technology which requires large inputs of labour and only becomes possible when there are many hands available.

The book is illustrated by a remarkable series of 'before' and 'after' photographs. The 'before' shots show landscapes scarred by erosion, supporting little but scrub. The 'after' shots show the same landscape now supporting crops and many trees. Indeed, one of the most surprising findings is that population growth can mean more trees.

This important study looks in detail at every aspect of the population/environment equation, including crops, technology, trees, livestock, income and investment, and ends with a radical re-assessment of the role of population growth in development. The authors argue that development can hardly take place without population growth, because it is this extra pressure on resources which forces people to adopt more efficient technology.

'It appears to be beyond doubt that low levels of population density

YES, POPULATION CERTAINLY IMPROVED OUR CHILDREN'S ENVIRONMENT – AS SOON AS THEY WERE OLD ENOUGH THEY LEFT HOME!

are inimical to technology change. Access to markets and knowledge depends on social and physical infrastructure, especially roads, schools and extension. The per capita cost of provision remains high until there has been quite a marked increase in density . . . At low densities, communication, both intellectual and physical, is difficult and the market for most products is limited.'

They also issue a timely warning to those who want to make Third World families smaller in the supposed interests of the environment:

'The provision of family planning information and the making accessible of supplies can be justified as adding to people's choices and the control which they have over their circumstances.

'To argue for population limitation on environmental grounds weakens the case for it both theoretically and practically.'

Attack

Congratulations to Tiffen, Mortimore and Gichuki for showing that population growth can improve the environment, and that Third World parents may have very good reasons for choosing to have large families.

Of course, they can expect to be lambasted by the powerful population control bureaucracies for daring to question the fashionable orthodoxy.

When some of Michael Mortimore's views were printed in *The Guardian* he became the subject of a sneering attack by Jonathan Porritt in *The Daily Telegraph*. Porritt accused him of sitting in front of computers and failing to understand real problems. Nothing could be further from the truth. Professor Mortimore, in fact, has turned down offers of lucrative desk-based jobs in this country because he wanted to use his knowledge to serve the people of Africa, which he has done for nearly thirty years. He and his co-authors will have performed a most valuable service if they help Africans to resist attempts by white, Western pedants to tell them how many children they can have.

• The above is an extract from the publication *Human Concern*.

Birth control fails to stem China's growth

By Graham Hutchings
Life in Beijing

Despite draconian birth control policies, China's population will reach 1.2 billion next month, a target Beijing once hoped to delay until the year 2000 to alleviate a growing strain on resources.

Officials at the State Family Planning Commission now say they want to confine the population to 1.23 billion by the end of the year, 1.3 billion by the end of the century and 1.6 billion by the year 2040.

The latest targets will require continued rigorous adherence to the controversial one-child per family policy begun in the late 1970s.

The one-child policy has helped to slow population growth, but its effects have varied in different parts of the country and it has been accompanied by abuses. These include forced abortions, sterilisations and, in some rural areas, female infanticide by parents anxious for a son.

The scale of China's population problem is apparent from an interview with Dr Jiang Zhenghua in the *People's Daily*. From the time of the Xia – the first dynasty dating from the 21st century BC – it took China 4,000 years to reach a population of 100 million, he said. It then took a mere 80 years to double that figure.

Between 1949 and 1969 the population grew by 260 million, the population of the United States.

Dr Jiang said that on present patterns of consumption, China would be capable of sustaining a population of up to 1.7 billion. But he warned of a very damaging effect on economic development should the population exceed two billion.

The environment

The biggest environmental problems stem not from resource shortages, but rather from our growing need for space and our rising output of pollutants

Population growth has been a strong factor in these areas. Slowing population growth can be a major conservation measure in its own right. It could reduce carbon dioxide emissions by an amount equivalent to halting all current deforestation.

Three impacts, three factors

Humans impact on the environment in three main ways: through the resources they use, the wastes they emit and the space they take up for settlements and farms. The strength of the impact depends not just on human numbers but on levels of consumption and the technologies used to meet that consumption and to dispose of wastes.

Population and resources

The debate on the links between population and environment has traditionally focused on resources. Will we have enough land, water, energy or minerals to meet the needs and desires of future populations or will resources pose limits to our future growth?

Many individual countries will face limits of land and water. However, on a global level we are not likely to run short of the essentials for survival, provided we do not exceed 11.5 billion – the UN medium pro-jection for the year 2150.

Human adaptability allows us to get around many scarcities. When a particular resource grows scarce, we step up exploration and improve efficiency. For many minerals, known

reserves have actually *grown* over the decades, despite increasing use. Clearly this cannot go on for ever: most minerals will eventually become scarce. When they do, we shift to substitutes.

However, the future will tax our adaptability to the utmost. Assume that world population reaches the 11.5 billion projected for 2150. Assume, for the sake of illustration, that we were all consuming at current American levels. In that case, today's world copper reserves would be used up in four years instead of 41. Today's oil reserves would run

out in seven years instead of 41. Even if we could find new sources and substitutes fast enough, the globe would be laid to waste if resources were mined at that rate.

Pressures on natural habitats

One of our biggest impacts on the environment is the space we take up for farms, homes, roads and other needs. Growth in population means

growth in the area we dominate. The area is taken away from wilderness and wildlife.

In the tropics, some 15.4 million hectares (154,000 square kilometres) of forest were being cleared every year around 1990, or about one square kilometre every three minutes. This is a 36 per cent increase over 1980, and amounts to 0.8 per cent of the total tropical forest area.

Between 1973 and 1988, population increase accounted for about 79 per cent of the loss of forest in developing countries. This is the proportion of forest cleared for farms to feed growing populations, and for towns, roads, and work-places to accommodate them. The other 21 per cent was due to increasing food consumption per person, and to ranching in Latin America.

Expanding human territories swallow up all kinds of wildlife habitat – wetlands, grasslands, even marginal semi-arid and mountainous areas.

In 50 African and Asian countries studied by the World Conservation Union, there was a very close link between population density and loss of original wildlife habitat.

In the 10 countries with the highest habitat loss (averaging 85 per cent) population density averaged 189 people per square kilometre. In the 10 countries with the lowest habitat loss (averaging 41 per cent) average population density was only 30 people per square kilometre.

The waste mountains

The gravest environmental problems of the future will come not so much from what we use, as from what we waste. Solid wastes grow in volume as populations and incomes rise. Over a lifetime the average person in a developing country produces 150 times their body weight in waste; the average European 1,000 times; the average American 3,900 times. In developed countries, landfill sites are growing scarce, so the pressure to recycle and reduce waste is growing.

Liquid and gaseous wastes are much harder to deal with. They flow into the oceans and atmosphere, and the institutions needed to control these great global commons do not yet exist.

Run-off from fertilisers is a serious water pollutant. In rivers, lakes and coastal waters it leads to large amounts of algae which starve the water of oxygen, killing fish and other animals. Fertiliser use increases to meet growing demand for agricultural products. In developing countries, some 72 per cent of this growing demand between 1961 and 1985 was due to population increase, the rest due to growth in consumption per person.

The most serious environmental threats will come from climate change. Global warming is fuelled by population growth. Carbon dioxide, the major greenhouse gas, comes from the burning of fossil fuels and deforestation. Population growth stokes fossil fuel use. Over the period 1965–1989 population growth accounted for 42 per cent of the growth in carbon dioxide emissions by developing countries. Increased consumption accounted for the rest.

Future pressures

The environmental challenges ahead are daunting. According to the medium UN projection, the world population will almost double over the next half century. Consumption per person will at least double, even if it grows at the low 1.3 per cent a year of the recession-hit 1980s. The total impact of population multiplied by consumption will therefore rise by a factor of four or more.

This means technology will have to reduce the impact of our activities by at least 75 per cent just

to keep environmental damage at its present high level, let alone to reduce it. Clearly the task for technology would be made much easier by a reduction in population growth. This would provide enormous savings in wildlife habitat left undisturbed. The low projection for 2050 would swallow up 4.4 million square kilometres less wildlife habitat than the medium, even if we assume a very low land requirement of only 0.2 hectares per person (about today's level in Asia). The saving is almost equal to all today's forests in developing countries in Asia. The low projection would take up a massive 9.4 million square kilometres less land than the high projection. This is more than all the rainforests in Latin America today.

The impact on global warming would also be dramatic. By 2050 the low population projection would mean 9.3 billion tonnes less in carbon dioxide emissions than the medium projection.[1] In today's terms, this is equivalent to halting all current deforestation, plus a 13 per cent improvement in global energy efficiency.

Slower population growth could also mitigate the impact of global warming. A recent study found that if carbon dioxide levels doubled by 2060, and world population reached the UN medium projection, some 823 million people in developing countries would be at risk of malnutrition. Yet if we could achieve the UN low population projection, the malnourished would number only 481 million – 342 million fewer people in hunger.

Slowing population growth can thus be a very significant conservation measure in its own right.

Bibliography

Alternative population projections: United Nations Population Division, *Long Range World Population Projections*, United Nations, New York, 1992; FAO, *Forest Resources Assessment 1990*, Rome, 1993; Harrison, P., *The Third Revolution*, Penguin Books, London and New York, 1993.

[1] At current world average rates of carbon dioxide emission per person.

● The above is an extract from *Briefing Pack on Population and Development*. See page 39 for address details.

Population and food

From the Committee on Population and the Economy

Ever since the population control movement got into its stride in the 1960s one of the most frequently used scare stories has been the prospect of starvation and famine as a result of population growth. Paul Ehrlich began his famous book *The Population Bomb* (1968) with the words: 'The battle to feed all of humanity is over. In the 1970s and 1980s hundreds of millions of people will starve to death.'

This fear went right back to the famous *Essay on Population* by Rev Thomas Malthus in 1798, in which he had predicted famine as the inevitable consequence of population growth. Malthus believed that population grew geometrically (2–4–8–16, etc.) while food production grew arithmetically (1–2–3–4, etc.).

Malthus was quite wrong on this key point: food production is quite capable of keeping ahead of population growth. In 1965, Danish economist Ester Boserup published her landmark study *The Conditions of Agricultural Growth*, in which she argued that it is not increases in food production which cause population growth it is the other way around. Population growth – is necessary to force communities to abandon very primitive means of getting food, such as the hunter/gatherer lifestyle or inefficient farming practices like forest fallow, and take up more intensive methods like ploughing with livestock. As growing populations become more specialised (in other words, people do not all live off the land) farmers have a greater incentive to increase food production, as they will have larger markets to sell into. Population growth is a good thing as it propels communities forward, from primitive to developed lifestyles.

Events have proved Boserup to be right. Since the first publication of her book, the population of the world has nearly doubled, but food production has kept well ahead. Figure 1 shows food production per capita, that is to say the amount of food which would be available to each person in the world if it were divided equally, based on figures from the United Nations Food and Agriculture Organisation. There has been a rise of over 30% in the period 1951–92. This has occurred in spite of the fact that Western farmers are paid millions of dollars a year to keep land out of production. If these European and American farmers were to produce to their capacity, food prices would collapse as a result of the glut.

In November 1993 the World Bank produced *The World Food Outlook* which anticipated further improvements in the world food situation. Here are some of its conclusions:

'World food production has more than kept pace with population growth and rates of growth of food production show few signs of slowing. During the 1980s, world cereals production increased by 2.1 % per annum while population grew by 1.7% . . . prospects are very good that the 20-year period from 1990–2010 will see further gains.

'The World Bank's index of food commodity prices fell by 78% from 1950–1992 in constant 1990 prices.

'Both land and water are abundant according to most estimates . . . Only 11% of the world's land surface is currently used for agricultural crops, and by one commonly accepted estimate, the world's land and water use for agriculture could more than double.

'The proportion of the developing countries' population suffering from chronic undernutrition has declined . . . from 36% during the late 1960s to 20% during the late 1980s.'

The report concludes that 'If Malthus is ultimately correct in his warning that population growth will outstrip food production, then at least we can say: Malthus Must Wait.'

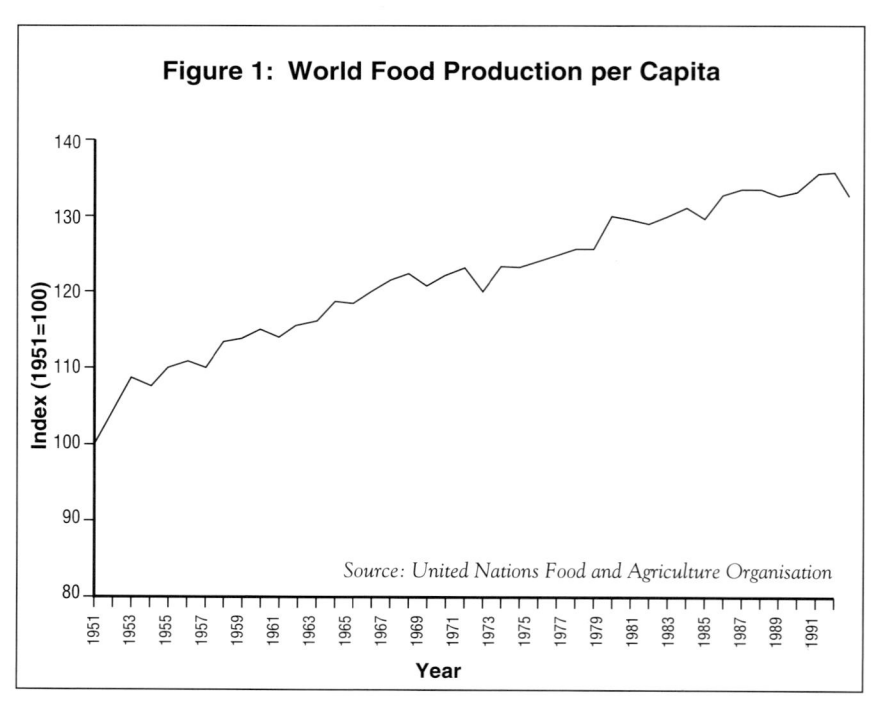

Figure 1: World Food Production per Capita

Source: United Nations Food and Agriculture Organisation

The problem of Africa

When we talk of increases in food per capita we are dealing in averages. In reality food is not shared equally between the peoples of the world, and when we break down the figures from the United Nations Food and Agriculture Organisation we see great variations between continents.

Figure 3 shows food production in Africa compared with Asia between 1961 and 1992. The disastrous performance of African countries is clearly dragging world averages down, as well as causing most of highly publicised famines. However this has nothing to do with 'overpopulation'. Asian countries have also experienced high rates of population growth and have achieved some of the highest population densities in the world, whilst still increasing food output per capita. Africa's problems stem from government programmes of intervention in agriculture which have been characterised by such crippling anti-market policies as the forced collectivisation of land, the establishment of monopoly purchasing boards for principal crops, the persistent underpayment of farmers and the favouring of urban elites. These have been coupled with chronic political instability in many countries, resulting in wars and civil wars. African famine is a political, not a demographic, phenomenon.

Even in Africa it is not all gloom. Where market mechanisms are allowed to operate, population growth and increased prosperity have gone hand in hand. In 1994 scientists from the Overseas Development Institute published *More People, Less Erosion*, a study of the Machakos district in Kenya between the 1930s and the present. Over the period population had increased by more than five times, but agricultural output had increased by about three times per head of population, and by ten times per hectare of land. The steepest increase had occurred in the period since 1977, when population density was increasing at its fastest rate with no new land available.

The population explosion

From Population Communications International

The greatest threat to humanity – indeed, the key to its fate – is the population explosion, warns Jacques-Yves Cousteau. The dean of ocean explorers, who has come ashore to broaden his message of an imperilled planet, scoffs at the current emphasis on so-called 'sustainable economic development' – the battle cry sounded at the 1992 Earth Summit in Rio de Janeiro. The 83-year-old aquanaut brands the concept an illusion and argues that what is a Western perception is not valid in a world of finite resources. He says that the promise of sustainable development cannot be delivered to 10 million people – Earth's projected population only 35 years from now. Cousteau now aims his conservation exhortations at lobbying international policymakers to redefine human progress. He complains of what he calls the hypocrisy of the freemarket system and condemns environmental destruction committed in the name of progress. Specifically, he cites such depredations as the draining of marshlands, the cutting of millions of acres of rain forest, and the destruction of coral reefs. Deploring the threatened eradication of entire populations of marine life by driftnetting and dynamiting, Cousteau says of his conservation concerns: 'I finally understood that we ourselves are in danger, not only the fish.'

(Press-Enterprise, 6 February 1994, Riverside, California). The above is an extract from *International Dateline*.

© *Population Communications International, 1994*

The future

In the 1950s and 1960s agricultural economists used to try to calculate the maximum number of people the world could support based on potential food production. The numbers ranged between 30 and 50 billion – when the global population now is less than 6 billion, and no one would seriously envisage this sort of increase.

In fact, rates of population growth are projected to fall by some 4000 by the year 2025. At the same time, there is every chance that agricultural yields will continue to rise thanks to advances in technology. The World Bank report mentioned above looks forward to the transformation of the former USSR and other Eastern European countries from net importers to net exporters of food. Those who demand population control must look to other arguments than food shortages.

• The above is an extract from the *Population Information Pack*.

© *Committee on Population and the Economy, February 1995*

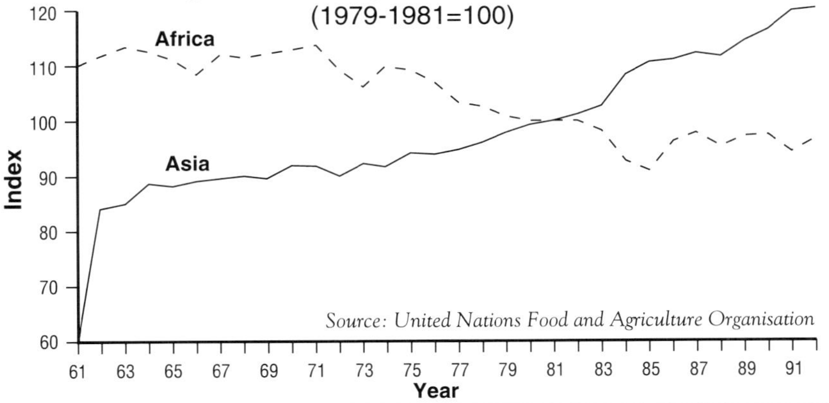

Figure 3: Per Capita Production Indices
(1979-1981=100)

Source: United Nations Food and Agriculture Organisation

The demographic slant

Plot the rise of world population on a graph, and you'll notice the slant levelling off, according to the latest estimates and projections from the United Nations

Our numbers are growing more slowly than expected, according to the Population Division of the UN Department for Economic and Social Information and Policy Analysis. Between 1990 and 1994, world population grew at 1.57 per cent per year, 'significantly' below the annual rate of 1.73 per cent which held for the preceding decade and a half and lower than the 1.68 per cent rate expected in 1992, when the figures were last revised.

The current rate is the lowest recorded since World War II and marks a return to the trend of declining growth prevalent from the mid-1960s to the mid-1970s.

At mid-1994, world population stood at 5.63 billion, an average increase of 236,000 people a day over the figure for mid-1993. Almost eight in ten – some 4.5 billion in all – lived in developing countries. The population of these countries is growing at a rate of about 1.9 per cent a year, compared to 0.4 per cent in the industrialized countries.

China, home to some 1.2 billion people, remains the world's most populous country, followed by India (919 million), the United States (261 million), Indonesia (195 million), Brazil (159 million), the Russian Federation (147 million), Pakistan (137 million), Japan (125 million), Bangladesh (118 million), and Nigeria (108 million). These are the only countries believed to have populations of more than 100 million. By 2050, they are likely to be joined by Egypt, Ethiopia, Iran, Mexico, the Philippines, Turkey, Vietnam, and Zaire.

India will replace China as the most populous country around 2045; by 2050, there will be 1.64 billion Indians and 1.61 billion Chinese,

according to the medium-fertility variant, or most likely projection.

At mid-1994, world population stood at 5.63 billion, an average increase of 236,000 people a day over the figure for mid-1993

Demographic changes are 'particularly striking' in Eastern Europe and the former Soviet Union, according to a Population Division statement. 'Many of those countries are exhibiting net losses of population (because of) very low levels of fertility, out-migration . . . and stagnating or rising mortality.' The statement also cites 'unexpected fertility declines which occurred in a number of high-fertility countries of sub-Saharan Africa and south-central Asia'. Indeed: 'In conjunction

with countries such as Kenya and Botswana, where fertility declines had been previously documented, evidence increases that a broad-based fertility decline may have begun in sub Saharan Africa. However, fertility remains very high in those countries and the future trends remain speculative.'

The '1994 Revision' shows fertility continuing to fall in, for example: Iran (from 6.8 children per woman in 1980–85 to 5.0 now), Bangladesh (from 6.2 in 1980–85 to 4.4), India (from 4.5 to 3.7), and Nepal (from 6.3 to 5.4).

The Population Division cautions that although population growth is slowing down, the most likely projections show world population growing to 7.5 billion people in 2015 and 9.8 billion in 2050.

For more information, contact: the Director, Population Division, Department for Economic and Social Information and Policy Analysis, United Nations, NY 10017, USA.

© Populi
September, 1994

Families plan a future of hope

A report on how the population explosion is being defused

For years, experts warned that the population explosion was catapulting the planet towards disaster.

There would be dire consequences for the environment and international stability, with the swollen population of the world's poorer nations enviously eyeing the rich West, so the theory went.

But the doomsday predictions have now been laid to rest – replaced by a far more optimistic vision of the future.

Population experts told at the weekend how family planning had brought about a 'reproductive revolution'. Most are now predicting that the world's population will begin to level off by the middle of the 21st century, bringing with it a dramatic decline in poverty.

Leading British expert Professor Malcolm Potts, based at the University of California, told a conference in Austria: 'The King of Thailand used to give gold medals every year to couples who had ten children. Now his birthday is a vasectomy festival.' Thailand is seen as a remarkable success story, with 66 per cent of couples using contraception compared with only 25 per cent 20 years ago.

Pramilla Senanayake, assistant secretary-general of the London-based International Planned Parenthood Federation, said the last quarter of this century had seen a global reproductive revolution.

'After decades of hard struggle to have family planning accepted as a basic human right, the reality of every child born being a wanted child suddenly seems to loom on the horizon,' she said.

By Jenny Hope and Tony Halpin

Family planning and education for women were the key factors in ensuring the revolution continued, the conference was told. In countries where no females had a secondary education, the average woman has seven children, but when 40 per cent have such an education, the figure drops to three.

According to statistics presented to the conference, the proportion of couples practising family planning had risen from one in ten in the early 1960s to one in two by 1990.

'The number of children per woman in developing countries will

stabilise at between 1.5 and 2.1 between 35 and 55 years from now,' said Joseph van Arendonk, deputy executive director of the UN Population Fund.

'No one can deny the success of family planning programmes, which have recorded such an impressive decline in the fertility rate over the past 30 years – from 6.1 to 3.3 children on average today.'

Ok Pannenborg, of the World Bank, said slowing population growth was vital to helping release developing countries from the poverty trap, and to stemming the tide of mass migration from low-income to high-income countries.

Despite the long-term optimism, the global population is expected virtually to double to 10 billion by 2050, compared with today's 5.5 billion. Ninety-four per cent of the growth is expected in the less developed countries. But after the middle of the century, the population will rise far less dramatically, reaching a plateau of 11.6 billion by 2150.

Some experts say the UN predictions are too optimistic and are based on the experience of countries where greater prosperity has brought dramatic falls in the number of children, such as Kenya and Zimbabwe.

'If all countries behaved like that, then we would be well on the way to a stabilisation at 10 billion,' said Stephen Kinzett, a demographer at Cardiff University; 'But it is unlikely to happen that fast in less-developed countries.' He believes the total is likely to reach 12 billion or 13 billion.

© *Daily Mail*
June, 1994

Family planning and family health

From Population Concern

Every year about 500,000 women die in pregnancy or childbirth, leaving at least one million children without mothers.

Studies in Africa and Asia have found that 25% of all deaths among women aged 15–49 were due to pregnancy or labour complications. By comparison, in the United States this figure is less than 1%. About 99% of maternal deaths occur in the developing world. In Africa the maternal mortality rate (the risk of dying from pregnancy-related causes) is between 160 and 1,100 per 100,000 live births. If the maternal mortality rate is 500 per 100,000 live births and a woman has 10 children (this is common in Africa) then the chances of her dying due to childbearing are 1 in 20.

Too young

Teenage pregnancies account for 10-15% of births worldwide. Studies from all over the world show that the risk of complications of pregnancy and delivery are affected by a woman's age. It has been estimated that if only women aged 20-34 became pregnant, maternal mortality would be reduced by one fifth in Mexico, Thailand and Venezuela, and by about one quarter in Colombia and the Philippines.

In many societies the age that women have their children is greatly affected by the age at which they marry – the earlier a woman marries the more children she is likely to have. Customs on marriage age vary greatly around the world and those married before the age of twenty range from 10% in Europe to 40% in Africa.

Too close

Many women in the Third World have their children in quick succession. However, when a woman has pregnancies close together the likelihood increases that the pregnancy will end in miscarriage or that the infant will die. In Kenya, the DHS in 1989 shows that children born within two years of the preceding birth are more than twice as likely to die before reaching the age of one as children born after an interval of four years or more. Also, with close birth intervals the mother's health is depleted, as it does not allow her to recover her energy, and so maternal deaths are also high.

Furthermore, the older child may die as it is weaned from the breast too early because the mother is pregnant again.

Too close

Too short an interval between births steeply increases the risk to both mother and child.

Space between births	No. of infant deaths (per 1000 births)
Less than 1 Year	
1 to 2 Years	
2 to 3 Years	
3 to 4 Years	

From a WHO survey of over 6000 women in South India.

Too many

Studies show that the risks to mother and child are highest with the first birth, lowest with the second and third birth and rapidly rise again after the fourth birth. This is highlighted in countries like Kenya where women have, on average, eight children.

Too young

Children born to women under the age 20 are approximately twice as likely to die in infancy as children born to women in their mid-20s.

Age of mother	No. of infant deaths (per 1000 per live births)
Under 20	
20-24	
25-29	
30-34	

From a survey in Argentina

24

Family planning saves lives

Each year 500,000 mothers die worldwide, due to pregnancy related complications. But with timing and spacing of births through family planning, women are able to have children when they are best prepared, with clear health benefits for both mother and child.

There are an estimated 25 million abortions in the Third World each year, where in some countries as many as one out of three women have had an abortion. One estimate shows that as many as 168,000 women may die of illegal abortions in developing countries every year. In Latin America half of all deaths among pregnant women are due to illegal abortion.

By averting unwanted pregnancies – and consequently illegal abortions – family planning could certainly prevent hundreds of thousands of needless deaths per year.

The need for family planning

It is often assumed that women in developing countries have large families because they choose to. But according to the World Fertility Survey approximately half the world's women want no more children. Of these, only half have access to effective birth control methods.

● The above is from *Population – a comprehensive study*, available from Population Concern. See page 39 for address details.

© *Population Concern*
February, 1995

Thinking about family planning and women's lives

How can family planning help women meet their needs? Thinking about this question requires making some basic distinctions

Women's practical and strategic needs

Women's needs can be grouped into two categories – practical needs and strategic needs. Caroline Moser, writing about women and development, defines practical needs as what women need to perform their conventional roles more effectively, such as good child care, better agricultural technology, and better housing. To help meet women's practical needs, women and program planners first analyse women's current activities and then develop ways to help women undertake those activities more effectively and with less burden.

In contrast, strategic needs are what women need to broaden their choices and opportunities. Although circumstances vary in different societies, strategic needs often include training for new jobs, enforcement of equal legal rights, and access to more education. Program planners try to help women meet their strategic needs by looking at the social factors that limit women's choices and then developing opportunities for women to assume new roles and responsibilities.

Practical and strategic needs are not mutually exclusive. Some new opportunities, such as the opportunity to control one's own fertility, help women meet both kinds of needs.

Contraceptive use and family planning services

The term 'family planning' often encompasses two distinct concepts – contraceptive use and family planning services: contraceptive use, of course, is use by an individual or couple as a means to avoid pregnancy. Contraceptive use helps women meet their practical and strategic needs by enabling women to control when and how many children to have.

Family planning services are organised sources of contraceptive methods. Such services include family planning programs of various types, retail sales of contraceptive supplies, and private practitioners' services. The foremost way that family planning services help to meet women's needs is by providing contraceptive methods safely and effectively, thereby enabling women to control when and how many children to have. In the course of providing contraception, however, family planning programs can do more. Program planners can deliberately design services to help meet women's strategic needs.

● Source: McCauley, A.P., Robey, B., Blanc, A.K., and Geller, G.S., *Opportunities for women through reproductive choice*, Population Reports, Series M, number 12, Baltimore, John Hopkins School of Public Health, Population Information Program, July, 1994.

© *Population Reports*
July, 1994

Putting the 'universal' into human rights

by Rebecca Cook

In the struggle for reproductive rights, victories are hard won. To win their rights, women have had to coax, appeal to, and do battle with men and the societies they've built at virtually every level, from basic beliefs to legal systems. They have had to overcome patriarchy, unequal opportunities in education and other means of empowerment, and various forms of physical violence such as rape and sexual harassment.

Yet, the struggle's gains are being withheld by intransigent state bureaucracies and legislative zealots in various industrialised and developing countries.

Women continue to suffer widespread disadvantages through governmental neglect of their reproductive rights. This is a violation of human rights embodied in international law, although with few exceptions a woman's right to control over her own sexuality and fertility is seen simply as one of a number of 'women's issues.' Neglect of preventable causes of reproductive ill health and pregnancy-related death is an affront to human dignity and is part of a larger, systemic discrimination against the 'other half' of humanity.

If international human rights law is to be truly universal, it must be applied both to require states to take effective preventive and curative measures to protect women's reproductive health and to afford women the capacity for reproductive selfdetermination.

International human rights treaties, including the Convention on the Elimination of All Forms of Discrimination Against Women, also known as the Women's Convention, require governments to ensure that women:

- are free from all forms of discrimination
- achieve their rights to liberty and security, to marriage and foundation of families, to private and family life, and to increased information and education and
- have access to health care and the benefits of scientific progress.

The right to regulate one's fertility – reproductive self-determination – under international human rights law is a composite right founded on these separate rights.

Photo: IPPF / Jeremy Hamand

The good news is that some countries are getting the point. Maria Isabel Plata of Profamilia, a Colombian non-governmental family planning organisation, explains that the women's movement successfully lobbied for incorporation of the principles of the Women's Convention into the country's 1991 Constitution, which provides for the right to decide, freely and responsibly, the number of one's children. Within this context, women are seeking new laws and policies for the promotion of their reproductive health. In 1992, the Ministry of Public Health issued a statement saying it considered 'the social discrimination of women as an element which contributes to the ill health of women'. A 1992 ministerial resolution orders all health institutions to ensure women the right to decide on all issues that affect their health, their life, and their sexuality. It guarantees their right 'to information and orientation to allow the exercise of free, gratifying, responsible sexuality which cannot be tied to maternity' and requires provision of a full range of reproductive health services, including infertility services, safe and effective contraception, integrated treatment for incomplete abortion, and treatment for menopausal women. And it emphasises the need for special attention to women at high risk of reproductive ill health, such as adolescents and victims of violence.

The bad news is that most states have fallen far short of ensuring reproductive self determination, as is apparent in policies that require husbands' authorisation for their wives to obtain contraceptive services.

The right to reproductive self-determination includes the rights to liberty and security of the person and the rights to receive and impart information. High rates of maternal mortality and morbidity are an obvious violation of the right to liberty and security of the person. The violation occurs when states deny women access to means of fertility control, and leave them at risk of unintended pregnancies.

The rights to impart and receive information are protected by, among other treaties, the European Convention on Human Rights. In 1992, the European Court of Human Rights found the Irish government in violation of these rights in the case of Open Door and Dublin Well Woman v. Ireland, which tested a governmental ban on counselling Irish women about abortions abroad. This same court has also held that states that require compulsory sex education in their public schools are protected by the European Convention, provided that the sex education curriculum 'is conveyed in an objective, critical, and pluralistic manner'.

Other elements of the right to reproductive self-determination include the rights to health care and the benefits of scientific progress. The Committee on the Elimination of Discrimination against Women, which monitors the implementation of the Women's Convention, questions member governments as to whether they are providing comprehensive reproductive health services and if not, whether they are violating women's rights to equality in health services. Moreover, governments that are not moving to provide modern, safe, effective, and acceptable methods of fertility control increasingly are being challenged to do so. In the case of the French abortifacient RU 486, for example, groups in Australia, Canada, Germany, New Zealand, and the United States argue that the manufacturer's refusal to seek approval to market the pill violated women's right to the benefits of scientific progress – a right protected by the International Covenant on Eco-nomic, Social, and Cultural Rights.

International protection of women's reproductive rights requires that governments eliminate all obstacles to reproductive self-determination and provide the necessary reproductive health services. In the struggle to hold on to the gains made by earlier generations of advocates and to finally put the 'universal' into human rights, victories will remain hard won.

● Rebecca Cook is an associate research professor and director of the International Human Rights Programme at the University of Toronto in Canada. This article first appeared in the December 1992/January 1993 issue of *Populi*.

© *Populi*
July/August 1994

Oxfam, family planning and population

The population question

For some years, rapidly growing populations have been a feature of many developing countries. Recent fears about the earth's environment have revived concern about the issue of population.

Population growth, poverty and environmental problems are interlinked, but the relationship is complex. It is not simply a matter of more people meaning more of the world's resources are being used up. A child born in a rich country will do far more damage to the environment during his or her lifetime than a child born in a poor country. This is because people in rich countries use far more of the world's natural resources.

We in Britain and Ireland often find it difficult to understand why poor people in developing countries have large families. One reason is because, in rural areas, people have little to rely on other than their families. Children start contributing to the household income from an early age, labouring in the fields or doing other work. And a large family means there is someone to look after you in old age.

The low social status of many women is another important factor. Women who have the benefit of education, and whose views and wishes are taken into account by their communities, are usually more self-confident and tend to have fewer children. Women's health is as important because this affects the chances of their children surviving. The healthier a woman's children, the fewer she needs to have to ensure the support of the family in later life.

Despite the pressures to have larger families, many poor people do want to limit the size of their families. They are prevented from doing so by the lack of access to contraceptives and family planning advice. An estimated 100 million women in the developing world would use contraceptives if they could get them.

Poor countries with an unfairly small share of the world's wealth find it difficult to meet the challenge of growing populations. They have few funds to support health and education services, or to finance schemes to alleviate poverty. At the same time poverty itself is resulting in more and more children being born. It is a vicious circle which rich countries must help to break.

Facts and figures

- At least half a million women die from pregnancy-related causes each year. The average risk of a woman dying as a result of pregnancy in a country like Britain is between one in 4,000 and one in 10,000. For a woman in a developing country the average risk is between one in 15 and one in 50.
- The industrialised countries of the North, which contain only 20% of the world's population, consume 80% of the world's resources.
- Women are having fewer children than 20 years ago In developed regions child-bearing rates have dropped from 2.6 to 1.8 births per woman, and in the developing world from between 5 and 7 children to 3–6.
- The unmet need for family planning is reflected in the huge number of illegal abortions – estimated at 50–70 million per year – mostly in developing countries.
- The United States has 6% of the world's population but consumes 30% of the world's energy. India, with 20% of the world's population uses only 2% of the world's energy.

Sources: *The World's Women: Trends and Statistics 1979–1990*, United Nations (1991); *No Time to Waste: Poverty and the Global Environment*, Dorothy Myers and Joan Davidson, Oxfam (1992); *Women and Health*, Patricia Smyke, Zed Books, 1992; *New Internationalist*, January 1990.

Oxfam and family planning

Oxfam believes that it is the right of individuals, particularly of women, to be able to choose the number of children they want, when to have them, and when to stop having them. Family planning is one means of

enabling women and men to choose what kind of contraception, if any, is suitable for them.

The best way for people to get a safe and dignified service is through basic health programmes grounded on an understanding of people's needs, where local Oxfam staff have built up good relationships with people at a grassroots level.

Oxfam spends about 15% of its annual overseas budget on health care and health education programmes, of which family planning is a significant part. A high priority is also given to education, literacy, income generation and other work which supports women in the process of taking more control over their lives. When women gain confidence in this way, they are in a better position to demand the services that they need.

Oxfam is particularly concerned that the uptake of family planning services be voluntary; experience has shown that coercive birth control programmes are often unsuccessful and counter-productive.

Poor, powerless and pregnant

Women are the traditional carers and health providers in developing countries. They also work in the fields and factories, sell goods at market, rear livestock, or work from home to bring in additional income. Often back-breaking and boring, their work is usually undervalued and taken for granted. They are also generally deprived of the chance to participate in decision making, which in many societies is strictly the realm of men.

In addition to these burdens, women are also responsible for the survival of their children. For many women, pregnancy is a yearly event, clearly limiting their potential contribution to the community as well as affecting their health and the welfare of their families.

In small ways, in many countries, things are beginning to change. Local organisations, with the support of agencies like Oxfam, are recognising the importance of women in the development process. Through women's groups, education and literacy projects, income generation and agricultural work, or mother and child health care, women are gaining confidence as decision makers, workers, carers, household managers and ultimately, as controllers of their own fertility. There's still a long way to go – but projects like these are an important catalyst for long-term change.

Further reading

- *Women and Health*, Patricia Smyke, Zed Books, 1992.
- *The Right to Choose: Pioneers in Women's Health and Family Planning*, Perdita Huston, IPPF/ Earthscan, 1992.
- *Poverty and Development in the 1990s*, Tom Hewitt and Ines Smyth, Open University, 1992.
- International Planned Parenthood Federation (IPPF) 1952-1992, Press Kit.
- *No Time to Waste: Poverty and the Global Environment*, Dorothy Myers and Joan Davidson, Oxfam, 1992.

© *Oxfam*
May 1994

The need for family planning support

Family planning, reproductive health care, female education and mother and child health are the best aid investments available. That is true whether the aim is to help poorer nations and disadvantaged groups to improve their incomes and quality of life or to safeguard peace, prosperity and a stable environment

Southern perspectives

Development

Experience has disproved the old theory that development is the best contraceptive. Birth rates do not automatically drop as incomes rise, but they do drop when investment is made in family planning, health, education, and women's status. Countries that followed this path have seen their fertility rates drop quickly and enjoyed a pay-off in faster economic growth.

Countries which invest in education, health and family planning perform best economically.

Human rights

Family planning is a human right recognised in international declarations since 1968. It is also a means of achieving other important rights such as the right to life, the right to improved health and the right to education.

Northern perspectives

Expanding the world market

Recent years have seen rapid economic growth in East Asia, but a rise in unemployment in Europe. The total world market is limited by poverty in South Asia and Africa and by slow growth in the Middle East and Latin America. Helping to foster human development will speed growth and in turn will expand the world market for goods and services to the benefit of North and South.

Migration

If the population of developing countries grows as projected, the pressure to migrate from the countryside

to urban areas and to richer countries will increase. Family planning and human resource development can help reduce migration pressures by lowering the rate of population growth and stimulating economic growth.

Security

Violent conflicts within developing countries have been increasing in frequency. Population pressures were a contributory factor in 27 out of 101 conflicts between 1940 and 1980, according to one United Nations Population Fund study. The link is no coincidence, for these are also the areas where competition for land, water and other resources is most intense.

Environment

Rapid population growth threatens not only national environments, but resources common to the whole globe.

High northern levels of consumption are a large part of the problem and the North must take measures to curtail these patterns. The North should not attempt to put the brakes on consumption growth in developing countries which are entitled to enjoy the same standard of living as the North, but it can help to slow population growth by helping to fund human development.

Making a difference

Increased effort in family planning leads to a decrease in the fertility rate. If all developing countries and aid donors gave high priority to human resource development, we could achieve the UN low population projection.

By the year 2000, this figure is only 168 million lower than the medium projection in 2000. By 2050 the gap has widened to 2.2 billion - equal to the whole world's population in 1950. Investing in human development can literally make a world of difference.

Bibliography

Costs: World Bank, *Effective Family Planning Programmes*, Washington DC, 1993; population and conflict: Choucri, N., *Multidisciplinary Perspectives on Population and Conflict*, Syracuse University Press, 1984.

● The above is an extract from *Briefing Pack on Population and Development*.

Family planning myths

From Save the Children

Myth 1

Birth control is a moral, personal and religious matter and charities should not interfere

Save the Children supports the right of everyone to make decisions about the size of their family. It believes in listening to what women want and need in their particular circumstances, and encourages them to make choices that are the best for them. Save the Children is most concerned that reproductive health programmes take into account people's culture and conscience. However, to make a choice women need good reliable advice, access to health services, better education and greater economic power. These are not moral or religious matters but questions of fundamental human rights.

We know that in certain parts of the world there is a large unmet need for family planning services. Save the Children believes that those needs should be met, and that such services are most valuable if delivered alongside related services that focus on health and women's rights, education, status and economic independence.

Save the Children's work is always delivered from the perspective of children's rights. That cuts across all boundaries of faith, religion and race.

● The best family planning programmes are tailored to the needs of the local community and are integrated with other services on offer. Pennywell Neighbourhood Centre in Sunderland (jointly funded by Save the Children, the local health authority and city council) offers a range of health services which includes a family planning clinic, pregnancy testing and ante-natal care. People drop in to use one service and take advantage of others at the same time. For example, young men come along to the male contraceptive clinic and may get involved with the men's group or take their children to be weighed at the baby clinic. 'We give out condoms with the baby milk!' says the centre's nurse.

● Where the majority of people are unable to read, it would be foolish to rely on education materials based on posters and leaflets. So, in rural Mali, Save the Children works with a group of musicians. Health staff produce information on family planning and other health issues; the musicians translate it into song. By the end of the performance the lead singer has made sure the audience knows what a condom looks like – and just how crucial it is in the prevention of pregnancy and AIDS/HIV.

Myth 2

Concern about family planning is a Western concept that is inappropriate and unwelcome in traditional societies.

It is true that many modern contraceptives were developed in the industrialised West. But it is completely wrong to suggest that family planning is a Western concept. Traditional societies have always had birth spacing methods. Traditional birth attendants help in delivering children and advising women on how to delay further pregnancies.

Women, wherever they may be, can be delighted to get access to family planning and other health services – however joyful their experience of having children. 'Now I've stopped having babies,' confirms Wasendi, a Save the Children-trained traditional midwife from south-east Pakistan. After having seven children, she says: 'Now I've had family planning – I use the Copper T coil. What does my husband think about that? He is very happy!'

It can be a cause for concern when unwanted imports from the West interfere with traditional birth control methods. For example, the widespread and often unethical promotion of baby milk substitutes can discourage breast-feeding – a natural way of spacing children. The basic principles behind Save the Children's work ensure that health and family planning services are never 'donor driven': that is, they meet the needs of the community, not of the agency providing the services. The drive to provide contraception should not take priority over provision of an integrated health service.

● Age-old traditional methods of birth spacing include the use of plant infusions (by the Navajo, Shoshoni and Hopis of North America and by women in the central forests of

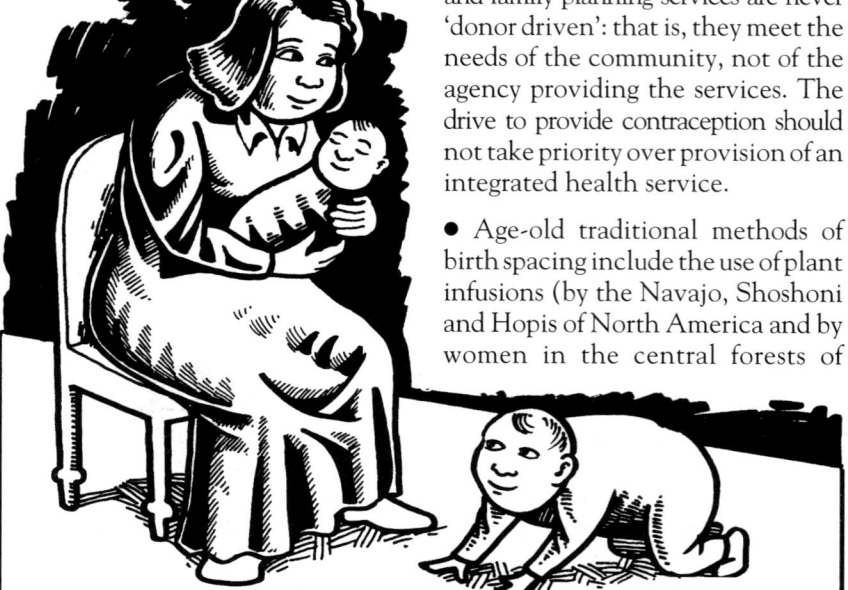

Paraguay), as well as social means – usually physical separation. In Ethiopia, it is common for a mother to go home to her parents after she has given birth for a 40-day period of seclusion and 'fattening' on ghee (clarified butter) and other rich foods.

● On Pemba Island, Zanzibar, women say they have agreements with their husbands to refrain from sex for two years 'because the baby is still young'. Others say they try to make themselves unattractive by shaving their heads or not using perfume. In West Africa, women go to maribouts (traditional healers) for contraceptive 'jujus' – written spells, sewn into leather pouches and worn round the hips, or used in a liquid form for ritual washing.

Myths are dangerous

Often based on fear and ignorance, they can fuel prejudice . . . or worse. This article has exposed some of the common misconceptions. It has also shown that the detailed picture can be complex and confusing. Luckily the underlying themes are simpler. There is one consistent message running through this article: it is that today's children and those who care for them have the right to make decisions about their lives free from the oppressions of poverty, poor education, disease and inadequate health care. If you want to help Save the Children, or find out more about its work, do not hesitate to contact us.

● The above is an extract from *Population Myths*, a free booklet available from Save the Children. See page 39 for address details.

© *Save the Children*
1995

24 volunteers sought to test first male contraceptive pill

The first contraceptive pill for men is to be tested in Manchester later this year, it was announced yesterday.

Doctors at St Mary's Hospital are seeking 24 volunteers to take the pill each day for six months, together with a weekly injection. Their sperm count will be checked each month to see whether the pill is working.

Dr Amanda Bellis, clinical research fellow at St Mary's, said the pill would contain a progestogen drug called desogestrel, which acts on the pituitary gland to inhibit the release of hormones responsible for the production of sperm

She said a weekly injection of testosterone, the male sex hormone, would also be given because the pill might otherwise cause the loss of all male sexual characteristics, such as facial hair growth.

'The need for an injection once a week may put some men off this method of contraception, and we shall be considering the possibility of a longer-lasting injection so that it does not have to be given so often,' she said.

The study would be carried out for six months on three groups of men, aged 19 to 45, to compare the effect of different doses of the pill.

Dr Bellis said that bigger trials at several centres would follow if the first trial showed that the method worked, was acceptable to the volunteers and had no side effects

'We are telling the volunteers that they should not regard this as a reliable method of contraception for the time being. If they have a partner they should use their normal contraceptive method,' she said.

The effects of desogestrel on sperm production would be reversible, with sperm counts expected to return to normal after six months, she added.

Trials have already been carried out on weekly injections of testosterone which is effective, by itself, as a male contraceptive.

More than 700 couples from nine countries took part in the trials and a study published in the *Lancet* in 1990 found only one pregnancy occurred in 12 months.

Men regained their fertility levels four months after the treatment was stopped and the main side effect was spots.

Dr Fred Wu, consultant physician at Manchester, who is in charge of the latest trial, said that some men developed acne and a slightly oilier skin as a result of testosterone injections.

He believes that the advent of a reliable male contraceptive will fundamentally alter attitudes as to who takes the burden for family planning.

However, it remains an open question as to whether women will feel able to rely on their partner's assurances that they have taken their pill.

© *The Telegraph plc*
London, 1994

Birth control monitor gets green light

By Roger Highfield, Science Editor

A natural method of contraception which relies on monitoring fertility has been hailed as potentially the most significant advance in birth control since the Pill.

A hand-held monitor that takes readings from disposable urine 'dipsticks' displays a green light during the safe period and a red light when a woman is fertile – normally eight or nine days every month.

The fertility monitor, the size of a spectacles case, measures changes in the wavelength of light absorbed by a dipstick, which is coated with antibodies that bind with two hormones found in urine.

The monitor also stores information on hormone level changes for the past six months, to take account of how the fertile period varies among individual women.

Early trials indicate better than 90 per cent effectiveness, roughly equivalent to barrier methods of contraception. The method has been given a cautious welcome by both the Family Planning Association and the Roman Catholic Church. A team from Exeter University is now co-ordinating nationwide trials of the system, which has taken 15 years to develop by Unipath, a subsidiary of Unilever.

'It is revolutionary – the biggest development in 20 years,' said Professor Bob Snowden of Exeter University, who is leading the year-long tests at his unit, the hub of the British family planning research network.

The unit is now recruiting women for the trials, which will compare the method with natural family planning, condom and cap. Other trials have started in Ireland and Germany, involving more than 1,200 women in all.

The attraction of such a method is the lack of side-effects. If the results are as promising as the laboratory tests suggest, it will be in use by the end of this year.

'It is aimed at the middle class, middle-aged woman who does not want to take drugs,' said Prof Snowden.

A Family Planning Association spokesman said: 'It is not going to take over from the Pill but it seems a very useful device.'

© The Daily Telegraph plc
London, 1995

Pop watch

Minor improvements

Birthrates among 15 to 17 year old girls have declined for the first time since 1986, reversing what had been a rapid increase in the late 1980s, federal health officials recently reported.

The National Center for Health Statistics (NCHS) said rates fell by 2 percent in 1992 – the most recent year for which statistics are available – after a 25 percent increase from 1986 to 1991.

The officials attributed the decline of births to better contraceptive use among teenagers and a leveling off of teenage sexual activity. Despite the decrease, the United States still has the highest rate of teen pregnancies among industrialised countries.

Male sterilisation

In an effort to boost male sterilisation, Mexican government health clinics are offering free, no-scalpel vasectomies that will soon be available throughout the nation. Since 1990 at least 45,000 men in Mexico have been sterilised. According to the Association for Voluntary Surgical Contraception, some 10 million men in the United States and 40 million elsewhere have had vasectomies. In comparison, at least 140 million women worldwide have been sterilised.

© The ZPG Reporter
January/February, 1995

Choice, choice, choice

The State of World Population 1994

A woman's reproductive choice is essential to the success of any population programme – more so than targets, quotas, or technology, according to this year's State of World Population Report from UNFPA. The Report places individual choice at the centre of population planning and notes that contraceptive and number-driven programmes are 'doomed to failure.'

The key to slowing population growth is support for reproductive freedom and the removal of social, economic, and political obstacles to family planning services, according to the Report. 'Choice begins not with technology but with an idea – the idea that every woman should have the right and the ability to decide whether and when to become pregnant,' it states.

But for this to happen, the narrow focus of traditional population and family planning programmes must be expanded and integrated into broader social and economic development goals.

The move towards population policies that support women's decision-making takes centre stage at this month's International Conference on Population and Development (ICPD), where leaders are expected to adopt a 20-year plan of action linking population and development goals with the overall aim of stabilising the world's population – currently estimated at 5.6 billion – at 8.5 billion by 2025.

According to the Report, the first step towards more effective population programmes is the positioning of family planning services within a wider range of reproductive health services. It argues that improvements in women's health would open up a range of options regarding education, marriage, employment, housing and migration: 'These options for personal development are development opportunities for the whole community.'

The Report says comprehensive, high-quality reproductive health services, with universal and completely voluntary access, improves the range of choices available to women and men. But it says the ability of women to actually make these choices requires communities and states to both reinforce a woman's personal sense of competence and control, and elevate her social status.

UNFPA Executive Director Nafis Sadik notes, however, that 'spouses, partners, and family members often limit the choices women are able to make with respect to childbearing, sexuality, schooling, nutrition, and other personal matters.'

To this end, she calls on policy makers to pursue the goal of 'gender security' for girls and women in order to preserve their rights to citizenship, employment, income, health care, and personal safety.

According to the Report, the concept of gender security should include freedom from childhood discrimination, nutritional deficiencies, and sexual and physical abuse.

Gender security also requires unhindered access to sexual and reproductive health care that includes services for sexually transmitted diseases and treatment of complications of unsafe abortion.

But UNFPA's call for gender equality in health, education, and the economic arena has been viewed with suspicion by some states and organised groups in the lead up to Cairo.

The most vociferous opponents to this approach are the Holy See and a handful of countries that have attacked the concept of reproductive rights – the cornerstone of the Cairo conference plan. They say the term implies a universal right to abortion on demand.

Still, the Report says that failure to create a context in which choice is permitted and encouraged will see only slow and marginal declines in overall population growth.

© Populi
September 1994

Photo: IPPF / Jeremy Hamand

A woman's reproductive choice is essential to the success of any population programme

A personal freedom

From Population Concern – working worldwide for basic healthcare and quality family planning

World facts

This is the first generation to know its children will not inherit a better world.

World population will double before today's teenagers become grey-haired. During the 90s an additional 97 million people are being added every year . . . almost a billion over the decade.

By the year 2000, half the population of the world will be under 24 years. There are now 30 million street children in the world.

Over 90 per cent of the population increase is happening in the developing world where this rapid rise is one of the driving forces of environmental change and poverty, and an obstacle to development.

At least one billion people are living in absolute poverty.

This pace of population increase in the developing world is matched by the massive levels of consumption by affluent nations, currently using 80 per cent of global resources.

The average person in an under-developed country leaves behind 150 times their weight in solid waste at the end of their lifetime . . . the average American leaves behind a mountain of waste 4,000 times their own weight.

Two billion people in 80 countries live in areas of chronic water shortage. Some of these countries are expecting their population to double in less than 25 years. Desertification is expected to affect more than a billion people by the year 2000.

Human needs

Women and men without family planning are forced to gamble with their future. This leads to unwanted pregnancies and also to millions of women resorting to illegal abortions

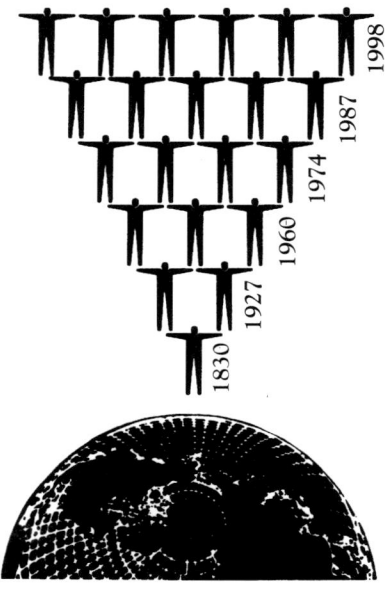

A growing concern
Each figure shown here represents 1 billion people

in an effort to cope. The impact of these unwanted pregnancies spreads from the individual to her whole family . . . affecting at present between 1.5 and 2 billion parents and children.

At least 300 million couples are still without access to the basic human right of planned parenthood.

Worldwide birth rates would fall by one third if all the women who want to space or halt their child-bearing could put this choice into effect.

Meeting the huge demand for family planning services will sub-stantially reduce population growth and improve people's lives.

500,000 women die needlessly every year from pregnancy-related causes.

A quarter of all pregnancies in the developing world end in abortion. In Eastern Europe and the

Commonwealth of Independent States there are 13 million reported abortions each year. The total world figure is about 50 million, legal and clandestine.

Half the women in the devel-oping world cannot read. Given some secondary schooling, a woman is 10 times more likely to use family planning.

Population milestones

AD 1: At the time of the Roman Empire the world population is believed to have been about 250 million.

1750: It took 1500 years for the global population to double to some 500 million, but as the Industrial Revolution gathered momentum, the world population moved into a faster pace of growth.

1928: Penicillin was discovered as the world population passed the 2 billion mark.

1974: Family planning became free on the NHS as the world population reached 4 billion.

1987: World population passed 5 billion as the first world conference on Safer Motherhood took place and issued a call for action to end the enormous toll of needless maternal death.

2000: Over 6 billion. Between now and the end of the decade Africa's population alone will increase by the size of the entire popu-lation of the United States, bringing its population to about 900 million.

2050: 10 billion people will inhabit the world, double the population of 1987.

Current U.N. estimates indicate world population will reach between 10.4 billion and 14 billion before it levels off.

© *Population Concern*
January, 1995

Population

Policies and programmes

Strong family planning programmes have the strongest effect where social and economic development is the highest. The Population Council has shown that among countries with a high level of development, a change in official family planning programme effort from 'very low' to 'high' produces an estimated additional decline in total fertility of 2.3 births per woman.

China: Is one child a wanted child?

From 1969/70 to 1977/78, China's highly successful family planning programme generated a rapid year by year decline in the annual number of births. Yet the controversial 'One-Child Policy' was initiated in 1979 as a means of supporting new economic targets for the year 2000. The aim of the population policy was to limit the maximum size of the country to 1.2 billion at the end of the century. However, the population has continued to grow more rapidly than the planners expected and in 1991 a new target of 1,294 million by 2000 was set.

Unlike almost any other society, China has the ability to introduce the concept of birth planning to each community. Every factory, rural village and township knows what the allocated number of births there are for each year and women are selected to meet those targets based on the number of years of marriage and whether they already have a child. The policy has been noticeably more successful in urban areas.

The actual implementation of the policy varies from area to area in China but generally speaking, if a couple have signed a one child certificate agreeing to have just one child the following measures are common: priority for housing, education and health allocation,

monthly payment of subsidies and higher pensions on retirement. If families sign the one-child certificate and then have additional children such facilities are removed and financial penalties are incurred. In certain areas, those of minority nationalities are allowed to have two children. Even for the majority Han people there are numerous circumstances in which a second child is allowed. For example in the urban areas, a second child is permitted (with at least a three year spacing period) if both parents are from single child families themselves.

The 'One-Child Policy' has thrown up some large and often controversial problems, particularly with regard to female infanticide which occurs mainly because many want their only child to be male. Abortion is freely available and there is some evidence that coercion exists when women become pregnant in an 'unplanned' way.

Continuing high acceptance rates for family planning and increases in the age of marriage coupled with the stated policies, means that by 2025 the population

growth rate will have declined to around 0.47% with an estimated population total of just over 1.5 billion. Although the Chinese government views this as too high, there are other very impressive gains that have been made in the last forty years such as a doubling of life expectancy at birth and a rise in literacy rates.

India: family planning or family welfare?

India has the fame of being the first country in the world to formulate an explicit population policy back in 1952. Despite this, population has nearly trebled from 361 million in 1951 and is projected to become the highest population in the world by 2050 with 1.7 billion people. For forty years India has been committed to population policies and programmes of various intensities. Measures which have been brought in include increasing the legal age at marriage from 15 to 18 for women and 18 to 21 for men; altering social benefits so they were related to a small family size; the compulsory involvement of all ministries/departments in family planning programmes; old age security measures; and, during the emergency period in the 1970s, mass sterilisation camps. It is with this last measure that India's population policy has become synonymous. Following vigorous incentive schemes which culminated in 10 million people being sterilised in just two years, the government led by Indira Gandhi was brought down. At the time many blamed the family planning programme but the real long term tragedy was the loss of credibility in community health services and a significant decline in the popularity of sterilisation.

The 1991 census recorded a population of 844 million. Consequently, the government of India has launched a new Family Welfare Campaign. (The term 'family planning' is no longer used because of the perceived links with sterilisation.) The Action Plan lists ten measures aimed at further reducing fertility levels such as a new package of incentive schemes, initiating family welfare innovations in urban slums, improving the quality and distribution of contraceptives, increased involvement of NGOs, increased culturally targeted information, education and communication (IEC) strategies, and strengthening political commitment at all levels.

The over-reliance on incentive schemes in the past is beginning to give way to a decentralised approach which reflects the vast social, cultural and economic differences between the states of India. However, targets such as increasing the contraceptive prevalence rate from 44% to 60% by 1995, and to decrease the growth rate to 1.25% by the same year seem unattainable at present.

Kenya: an African experience

Generally speaking, countries in Africa have been the last to adopt population policies. Until recently only a handful of countries had set out explicit policies and programmes but this has changed in recent years. Kenya was the first sub-Saharan African country to state a policy back in 1965, ten years after the formation of the Family Planning Association of Kenya.

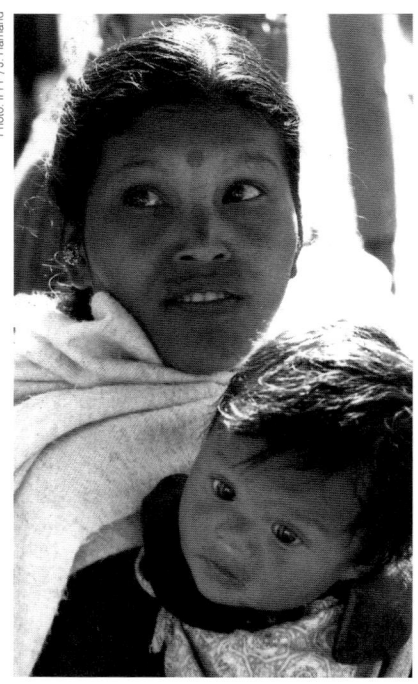

Photo: IPPF / J. Hamand

Despite this, Kenya continues to be a country with a rapidly expanding population, with fertility rates around 6.5 per woman following a decline from an all-time high of around 8.0 in the 1980s. Much of the programme effort is now being directed into information, education and communication (IEC), which coupled with the rapid modernisation of the country seems to be working. The latest surveys have indicated that ideal family size has declined to around 4.6 and that uptake of modern contraception is now 28% from 6% in the mid 1970's.

Current population policy goals in Kenya include to reduce fertility levels further and encourage Kenyans to 'have small families', to reduce internal migration which causes unplanned settlements, to motivate males to adopt family planning, to improve the status of women, to provide IEC to men, women and youth, to ensure the availability of contraception, and to improve the quality of the service provided.

However, it must be recognised that there is still a lack of real political commitment, high socio-cultural barriers and the predominance of a strong patriarchal society – all of which mean that fertility will remain fairly high for many years to come. This can be said for many parts of Africa.

Italy: the one child policy without force

In Italy there is no explicit government policy but the combination of implicit policies through social reforms and legislation mean that the country has the lowest fertility rate in the world at just 1.2. If fertility rates remain at this low level, the population of around 57 million will start to decline.

This level of fertility is all the more surprising as Italy is predominantly Catholic and has the Vatican and hence the powerful influence of the Pope within the country. Despite this influence and the fact that Italy maintains a stance not to intervene to alter trends and levels of fertility, legislation on women's rights, health policy and social reforms have had tremendous effects on the demographic situation in the country.

Various factors can be identified for the reasons behind Italy's low fertility: relatively high age of first marriage at 25 coupled with a very low rate of births outside wedlock of around 6% (compared for example with the UK which has 25%), delayed first birth and a preference by Italians for only one child, liberal contraception and abortion regulations (abortion is available on demand in the first three months of pregnancy), and growing numbers of women in the workforce giving rise to the opportunity cost of having children.

Abortion is used widely in Italy but the vast majority of abortions are carried out for married women (63%) and to those over the age of 25 (72%) – mainly the result of contraceptive failure. This tends to support the case for more substantial education on modern, effective methods of contraception.

Demographic matters of particular concern are immigration and spatial distribution. Immigration is rapidly becoming a concern in many developed countries because of the increasing refugee problem and requests for political asylum. Spatial distribution in Italy has become a matter of concern because of the growing numbers of people leaving the poorer South for the more prosperous North, especially to settle in the larger cities. It seems that the cost of children is increasing, and, with a fairly high unemployment rate, it is likely that the 'one child family' will continue to be the norm in Italy.

Pakistan: with all the will in the world . . .

Pakistan is a prime example of where a country has failed to succeed in its stated population policy aims. Like India, Pakistan acknowledged the strong linkages between population growth and development from the 1950s onwards, although it was not until 1965 that any real policies were put forward. A target-orientated approach was established in order to get relevant information to all couples and to provide contraceptive services to 20 million couples. However, it was found that only 6% of married women of reproductive age (15–49) were practising family planning.

Further Five Year Plans were disrupted by various political changes until the 1980s when a multi-sectoral approach to population policy was established. This entailed reorganisation of the bureaucracy including the transfer of the Population Welfare Division to the Ministry of Planning and Development and the establishment of the National Institute for Population Studies. In 1983 policies that were emphasised included: male responsibility, breastfeeding, late marriage, and improving women's status.

Since then the government has announced new measures to stress coverage of family planning programmes in the rural areas, strengthening of the motivational campaign, and forcing every health facility to provide family planning services.

Results of all these measures are disappointing: Pakistan's population increased from 49 million in 1960 to an estimated 115 million by 1991. During the same period total fertility hardly changed from a level of 7.0 to 6.75 children per woman. Results from the 1990/91 Demographic and Health Survey show the contraceptive prevalence rate amongst married women of reproductive age to be low at only 12% (although knowledge of any method is

---

In Pakistan it is questionable whether the people really want these policies and programmes

---

comparitively high at 78%). A number of reasons may be cited as to why policies have not worked in Pakistan such as lack of sustained political support and support from religious leaders, over-reliance on foreign aid, inadequate supervision, evaluation and monitoring of programmes, and the lack of an integrated approach.

In Pakistan it is questionable whether the people really want these policies and programmes. In this male-dominated society, one of the most important questions is the raising of women's status. It may be that lip-service has been paid to the formulation of population policies; for as long as donor money rolls in, the men of Pakistan can increase their wealth and control over the society in which they live. This is illustrated by the amazingly optimistic targets set by each successive five year plan. For example: the coverage of family planning in the rural areas is to be expanded from 5% in 1993 to 70% by 1998.

Thailand: the way to go . . .

If there is a success story of population policies and programmes in the world it is Thailand. Total fertility has declined from just over 6 in the early 1960s to 3.7 in 1980 and to the replacement level of 2.1 in 1991. This impressive decline in fertility was brought about at a very early stage by strong policy statements from the politicians who ensured appropriate programmes were formulated and implemented. Instrumental in this was the establishment of the National Family Planning Programme (NFPP) in 1970, which led to a rapid increase in the use of family planning from 15% in 1969 to nearly 70% in 1991.

Throughout the last thirty years Thailand has consistently responded

---

to the economic arguments for family planning. Compared to many other countries where policy has been framed under the health rationale for family planning, it seems that it was the consequences of population growth on the economy of the nation which held greater influence for the policy's success. A key part of this success has been the multi-sectoral approach taken in planning and implementing the policy and programme. Currently the policy focuses on six specific areas: population research, population and the environment, ageing, adolescents and youth, women in development, and HIV/AIDS.

Although Thailand's population policy has been referred to as an 'integrated' approach, it is essentially vertical. What distinguishes it from other policies is the attention paid to social development policies, such as education, and effective efforts to empower women. Thai women are amongst the most economically active in Asia. The female literacy rate is almost as high as the male literacy rate of 96%.

Furthermore, the primary school enrolment ratio for girls and boys is equally high at 85% and secondary school enrolment for girls is 28%, compared to 32% for boys. In 1980, a special task force was set up to formulate a long-term strategy into the next century for women's development at all levels.

Other lessons to be learned from Thailand's success include the importance of good infrastructure for effective service delivery, that family planning communication can be cost-effective if the mass media is controlled by the government, that mass promotion of a single contraceptive method can be dangerous, and that trained personnel (particularly female) are essential for the delivery of family planning, especially in rural areas.

• The above is an extract from *Population: policies and programmes* written by Steve Kinzett, Sir David Owen Population Centre, Cardiff University. Contact Population Concern for the complete document. Address details are on page 39.

© Population Concern 1994

INDEX

ADDITIONAL RESOURCES

You might like to contact the following organisations for further information. Due to the increasing cost of postage, many organisations cannot respond to inquiries unless they receive a stamped, addressed envelope.

Action Aid
Hamlyn House
MacDonald Road
Archway
London
N19 5PG
Tel: 0171 281 4101
Fax: 0171 281 5146
A charity working with children, families and communities to improve the quality of life in some of the poorest parts of the world.

Birth Control Trust (BCT)
27-35 Mortimer Street
London
W1N 7RJ
Tel: 0171 580 9360
Fax: 0171 637 1378
Publishes a wide range of books, pamphlets and reports on reproductive health including issues such as abortion, teenage pregnancy and sterilisation. A stamped, addressed envelope is required is seeking their publication list.

Central Broadcasting Ltd
Central House
Broad Street
Birmingham
B1 2JP
Tel: 0121 643
Fax: 0121 616 4259
Some of the material contained in this book was taken from the *Moving Pictures Bulletin* special issue on population, produced jointly by Central Television and Television Trust for the Environment.

Committee on Population and the Economy
13 Norfolk House
Courtlands
Richmond
Surrey TW10 5AT
Tel: 0181 948 6903
Produces *Population Information Pack*.

International Institute for Environment and Development
3 Endsleigh Street
London
WC1H 0DD
Tel: 0171 3888 2117

International Planned Parenthood Federation (IPPF)
Regents College
Regent's Park
London
NW1 4NS
Tel: 0171 486 0741
Fax: 0171 487 7950
An international federation of independent family planning associations in 134 countries. It aims to initiate and support family planning services throughout the world in the benefits of the whole family, particularly mothers and children, of spacing and planning births.

Marie Stopes International
68 Grafton Way
London
W1P 5LE
Tel: 0171 388 3034

Oxfam
274 Banbury Road
Oxford
OX2 7DZ
Tel: 01865 311 311
Produces a wide range of publication including free leaflets. Ask for their Resources for Schools and Youth Workers catalogue.

Population Concern
178-202 Great Portland Street
London W1N 5TB
Tel: 0171 631 1546
Fax: 0171 436 2143
Produces a wide range of material including data sheets, maps, posters, factsheets, videos, *People and Planet* – a quarterly magazine, and student packs. Forthcoming resources include a software pack on world population. Ask for their publications list. Population Concern, a charity, is currently working with local partners in 15 countries worldwide in South Asia, Africa, Latin America and the Caribbean to meet community demands for better healthcare and quality family planning.

Save the Children
2nd Floor
National Deposit House
1 Eastgate
Leeds LS2 7LY
Tel: 0171 703 5400
Produces a wide range of materials. Ask for their catalogue.

UNICEF
55 Lincoln's Inn Fields
London
WC2A 3NB
Tel: 0171 405 5592

United Nations Information Centre
18 Buckingham Gate
London
SW1E 6LB
Tel: 0171 630 1981

World Development Trust
25 Beehive Place
London
SW9 7QR
Tel: 0171 737 6215

Zero Population Growth (ZPG)
1400 Sixteenth Street N.W
Washington DC 20036
USA
Tel: (202) 332 2200
Fax: (202) 332 2302

ACKNOWLEDGEMENTS

The publisher is grateful for permission to reproduce the following material

Chapter One: Population

Overpopulation, © Population Concern, *Populous nations*, © Population Communications International, 1994, *Third world population growth*, © Population Communications International, 1994, *Global trends*, © Marie Stopes International, January 1995, *Tax parenthood to save the world*, © The Independent, 10th August 1994 page 2, *Population and fertility rates*, © Committee on Population and the Economy, January 1995, *Population Myths*, © © Save the Children, *The three culprits*, Moving Pictures Bulletin, Population Issue, © Central Television and Television Trust for the Environment (TVE), page 2, *The three impacts*, Moving Pictures Bulletin, Population Issue, © Central Television and Television Trust for the Environment, page 3, *Population: resources and the environment*, Population Concern 1994, *Why population growth improves environment*, © Human Concern – Society for the Protection of the Unborn Child (SPUC), Winter 1994 page 4, *Environment*, © Marie Stopes International, 1994, *Population and food*, © Committee on Population and the Economy, January 1995, *The population explosion*, © Population Communications International, 1994, *The demographic slant*, © Populi, September 1994 page 5.

Chapter Two: Family Planning

Families plan a future of hope, © The Daily Mail, 6th June 1994 page 12, *Family planning and family health*, © Population Concern, February 1995, *Thinking about family planning and women's lives*, McCauley, A.P., Robey, B., Blanc, A.K., and Geller, G.S.: Opportunities for women through reproductive choice, Population Reports, Series M, Number 12, Baltimore, John Hopkins School of Public Health, Population Information Program, July 1994, © Population Reports, July 1994, *Putting the 'universal' into human rights*, © Populi, July/August 1994, page 15, *Oxfam, family planning and population*, © Oxfam, May 1992, *Family Planning Myths*, © Save the Children 1995, *24 volunteers sought to test first male contraceptive pill*, © The Telegraph Plc, London 1994, *Birth control monitor gets green light*, © The Telegraph Plc, London 1994, 6th January 1995 page 9, *Pop watch*, © The ZPG Reporter, January/February 1995, *Choice, choice, choice*, © Populi, September 1994 page 4, *A personal freedom*, © Population Concern, 1994, *Population*, © Population Concern, 1994.

Photographs and illustrations

Pages 1, 8, 16, 17, 18, 22, 23, 28, 29, 31, 35: Ken Pyne, pages 3, 19: A. Haythornthwaite / Folio Collective, pages 4, 26, 33, 36: IPPF / J Hamand, pages 7, 25, 30: A. Smith / Folio Collective, pages 10, 13: K. Fleming / Folio Collective, page 12: Howard J. Davies / Panos Pictures, page 13: Greg Spalenka / Image Bank, page 15: Graphic News, page 34: Population Concern.

Craig Donnellan
Cambridge
May, 1995